CLEMATIS
a care manual

Mary Toomey

LAUREL
GLEN

First published in the United States
in 1999 by Laurel Glen Publishing
5880 Oberlin Drive, Suite 400
San Diego, CA 92121-4794
1-800 284-3580

First published in Great Britain
in 1999 by Hamlyn, a division of
Octopus Publishing Group Limited
2-4 Heron Quays, London, E14 4JB

ISBN 1-57145-637-6

1 2 3 4 5 99 00 01 02 03

Produced by Toppan
Printed in China

Publishing Director
Laura Bamford
Creative Director
Keith Martin
Executive Editor
Julian Brown
Executive Art Editor
Mark Winwood
Editor
Karen O'Grady
Production Controller
Clare Smedley
Picture Research
Wendy Gay
Photography
Sean Myers

North American Edition
Publisher
Allen Orso
Managing Editor
JoAnn Padgett
Project Editor
Elizabeth McNulty

Library of Congress
Cataloging-in-Publication Data

Toomey, Mary
Clematis : a care manual / Mary
Toomey. -- North American ed.
p. cm. -- (Includes biographical
references (p.) and index.)
ISBN 1-57145-637-6
1. Clematis. I. Title. II. Series.
SB413.C6T66 1999
635.9'3334--dc21   98-56392
CIP

Contents

Introduction

Introduction

As a general gardener with a special love for clematis, I have been growing these plants for well over thirty years in gardens of various sizes. It was my nature study teacher in primary school who drew my attention to the parachute mechanism used to disperse the seeds of *Clematis vitalba* (Old Man's Beard). Ever since then, my fascination with clematis has grown by leaps and bounds, and I ended up growing as many species and hybrids of the genus *Clematis* as possible. When I ran out of space for yet another clematis in my own urban garden, I began to grow them in borrowed spaces of my friends' and neighbors' gardens. Even though there were a few good books on clematis in 1968—the year I planted my first *Clematis montana* var. *rubens*, as a young student at university—there was not a lot of spare cash to splash out on specialist publications. I relied on the few gardening books available in my local library and adopted a scientific-botanical approach to growing clematis. These books were the means by which I learned about these plants and their requirements for successful growth and cultivation in the garden.

During the course of the past few years as the Editor of *The Clematis*, the journal of the British Clematis Society, I have been very privileged to meet many fellow members of the society who have cheerfully and generously shared with me their experiences of growing clematis. Over a long number of years I also met members of the gardening public at my lectures and horticultural shows up and down the country, and realized that many of them are often put off by the myths and mysteries of growing clematis.

The main aim of this book, then, is to address the problems that face gardeners who grow clematis and to engender a love for this very special genus of plants. Strictly speaking, this book is the summation of my personal experience, and that of many other able clematarians around the world, of cultivating and enjoying clematis in the garden.

The genus *Clematis* enjoys an almost world-wide distribution and the vast majority of plants are suited to most growing conditions. Most are hardy in the British Isles and United States. Clematis are climbers, with the exception of species and hybrids such as *C. heracleifolia, C. integrifolia, C. x aromatica,* and *C. recta,* which are herbaceous. The herbaceous species and hybrids thoroughly deserve a place in the perennial border.

Many clematis species and hybrids are widely available to the modern gardener and, if chosen with care, it is possible to have a clematis in flower for ten to eleven months of the year. Apart from the sheer beauty, form, size, and shape of the flowers, the seed heads of some clematis not only beautify the autumn and winter garden but are also welcome additions in flower arrangements.

The past few years have witnessed an unprecedented rise in the popularity of clematis as a garden plant. This is simply wonderful. However, despite the wide availability of some small-flowered species and hybrids, gardeners seem to prefer the large-flowered hybrids.

I agree that there are some superb large-flowered hybrids, old and new, which carry very handsome single and double blooms, in colors ranging from whites, blues, and pinks to vibrant and vivacious reds and purples, and it is easy to fall in love with them. May I appeal to gardeners to grow more of the exquisite and floriferous and often trouble-free small-flowered species and hybrids, which belong to the alpina, macropetala, viticella, tangutica, and texensis groups. Propagation of species clematis that are not widely available for sale from seed can be a great challenge and fun too.

Mary Toomey

History, Botany, and Nomenclature

History

In 1548, William Turner mentioned the earliest known species *C. vitalba* as the "Hedge-vine" in *The Names of Herbes*. The 16th century herbalist, John Gerard, having bumped into it in almost every hedgerow from Gravesend to Canterbury probably thought it would delight the passers-by and gave it the name "Traveler's Joy." It was also known as "Gypsy's 'bacca" (short for "tobacco") since country people dried the cut stems of the plant and used them for smoking. The downland shepherds called it bithywind or "Devil's Guts" and used the long woody stems from the hedges to repair broken and worn-out hurdles. The common name, "Old Man's Beard," of course refers to the fluffy seed heads.

Although it did not enjoy the prominence the rose received through the ages, clematis came into its own as far back as 1569 when the first species, *Clematis viticella*, was introduced into Britain from Spain, followed closely by *C. integrifolia*, *C. cirrhosa*, *C. flammula*, and *C. recta* from southern and eastern Europe. All four of these species are in cultivation today. After a flurry of activity there was a long pause of almost a century before the North American species joined European species in Britain. *C. crispa* was introduced in 1726, followed by the Leather Flower, *C. viorna*, in 1730. Soon afterwards, in 1731, *C. orientalis* arrived from northern Asia. Even though hybridization had not commenced at this stage, the second half of the 18th century ushered in a very important Chinese species, *C. florida*, which was to become the progenitor of a number of modern large-flowered garden hybrids. Other newcomers were *C. cirrhosa* ssp. *balearica* from the Balearic Islands and *C. alpina* from northeast Asia and central Europe. which arrived on the scene in 1783 and 1792, respectively.

The 19th century was an exciting era in the history of clematis. Many more foreign species of valuable clematis, including *C. patens* from Japan (1836), and *C. lanuginosa* from China (1850) were added to the list of earlier arrivals. These two species, along with *C. florida* (1776) and *C. viticella* (1569), opened the channels for hybridization.

Early Hybridization

The credit for raising and introducing the earliest known hybrid, in around 1835, must go to Mr. Henderson of the Pineapple Nursery, St John's Wood. The crossing of *Clematis integrifolia* x *C. viticella* resulted in *C. x hendersonii* which was later given the name *C. x eriostemon* 'Hendersonii.' Following the introduction of the first hybrid, many British and European nurserymen embarked on extensive programs of hybridization in earnest to produce some fine varieties of clematis. Thanks to the early dedicated work by Jackman's of Woking, Cripps and Sons of Tunbridge Wells, Charles Noble of Sunningdale, Bouamy Frères of Lyons, and many others, modern gardeners are blessed with some wonderful large-flowered and excellent small-flowered hybrids. Many of the outstanding old varieties of clematis are still in cultivation. However, with the onset of the disease "clematis wilt" around 1880, interest in clematis among nurserymen and gardeners alike began to wane.

Clematis Revisited

Over the first twenty-five years of the 20th century, William Robinson and Ernest Markham of Gravetye Manor fame were largely responsible for rekindling the interest in clematis and cultivating some marvelous plants, such as *Clematis tangutica* 'Gravetye,' *C. texensis* 'Gravetye Beauty,' *C.* 'Ernest Markham,' *C.* 'Miriam Markham,' *C.* 'Markham's Pink,' and others. Many plant collectors, too, were very busy at least until the First World War and some splendid new species, notably from China—*C. armandii*, *C. montana* var. *rubens*, *C. rehderiana*, and *C. chrysocoma* among others—were introduced. Shortly after the Second World War there was renewed interest in growing clematis in the British Isles, followed by a global revival in its popularity as a garden plant. Brand-new and exciting hybrids (cultivars) from all over the world arrived on the scene and were made available to the public by enthusiastic nursery growers.

The success story of this very versatile plant continued, and the British Clematis Society was founded in 1991 to promote the cultivation and preservation of clematis. The decade of the nineties certainly belongs to the genus *Clematis*, which includes sociable climbers and some choice herbaceous and sub-shrubby plants.

Classification

With so many species and hybrids available for sale, the gardener is faced with the dilemma of selecting types that can be made the most of in the garden. A careful choice can result in a clematis in bloom during almost every month of the year. Botanists and some gardeners who specialize in clematis are concerned with all the detailed characteristics of the plants and their classification. The general gardener, on the other hand, is interested in choosing the best clematis plants for the garden according to flowering times, shape, size, color, uses in the garden, and compatibility with other garden plants.

There no longer seems to be a clear-cut demarcation between spring and summer, or autumn and winter, or winter and spring. January and February may be unusually warm or April and May exceptionally cold. Terms such as early, mid-season, late, tend to cause a certain amount of confusion when applied to the flowering times of any plant. How early is early or how late is late? Early and late could easily vary between one part of the country and another. The gardener will have to decide the arrival and departure times of winter, spring, sum-

Clematis vitalba **is a wonderful vanilla-scented climber with prominent seed heads. It brings color and interest to hedges and fences.**

mer, and autumn. From the author's experience of growing clematis, as long as severe frost and extreme drought do not play havoc with clematis, most will cope with the vagaries of weather and even sudden wilt (see page 69), to come through in style.

Despite the changing weather patterns over which no gardener has any control, some background knowledge about the different groups of clematis helps gardeners to choose their clematis. Correct choice is important if the aim is to grow a clematis in association with other flowering plants and, in particular, roses.

Before considering the classification of clematis, it is helpful to know the differences between species, cultivars, and hybrids.

Species

"A group of related individual plants with certain common characteristic features, often found within a distinct geographical range." Members of a species can interbreed freely with one another, but not with members of another species. If they do, the resulting offspring are not fertile. In the Latin name of a plant there are two components: the first is the name of the genus (plural genera), which indicates a group of related but distinct species of plants, and the second the name of the species—for example, *Clematis montana, Clematis alpina.*

Cultivar

There are a number of different methods for selecting a cultivar. For example, a plant brought into cultivation from the wild may throw up a different form in the process of being grown and propagated in the garden. If this form retains its characteristic or combination of characteristics through growth and propagation, it can then be designated a cultivar. A cultivar may also be selected from a batch of seedlings, or a chance seedling found growing in the garden may be selected and introduced as a cultivar. In addition, when deliberate crosses are made between different species, the new plants, which are referred to as hybrids (see below), also arise in cultivation. Therefore, they can also be called cultivars. Examples of cultivars would be *Clematis alpina* 'Pamela Jackman' (seedling selected and introduced as a cultivar) or *C.* 'Hendersonii' (a hybrid obtained from a deliberate manmade cross and introduced as a cultivar).

Cultivars do not grow naturally in the wild. Cultivars should be propagated by layering, cuttings, division, or other appropriate vegetative means to maintain stocks. If propagated from seed, the plants will not "come true."

Hybrid

Hybrids may occur naturally as result of cross-pollination and fertilization between two species growing in the wild or in the garden, though they are more commonly manmade (deliberate crosses). Technically speaking, a hybrid is a mongrel. It is the result of cross-fertilization between two or more different species of the same genus: *Clematis viticella* x *C. 'Integrifolia* = *C. 'Hendersonii'* or *C. patens* x *C. lanuginosa* = *C. 'Lawsoniana.'* Since these hybrids were raised in cultivation by humans these are also cultivars. Hybrids do not breed true from seed.

The main distinction between a hybrid and cultivar is that all hybrids are cultivars, not all cultivars are hybrids. Generally speaking, species clematis are much tougher than the highly bred cultivars and less susceptible to diseases and are also less prone to attacks by garden pests.

Grouping or Classification

For convenience, the clematis we grow in our gardens can be broadly divided into climbers and nonclimbers. The climbers can be divided into two major groups: small-flowered species and hybrids; and large-flowered hybrids.

The small-flowered species are those introduced into garden cultivation from the wild and are natives of many regions of the world. Hybridizers used some of the beautiful small-flowered wild clematis species to produce a number of exciting hybrids. The large-flowered hybrids are the result of deliberate man-made crosses between the wild clematis that were introduced from Japan and China a long time ago. More and more large-flowered hybrids became available as a result of crossing and re-crossing a number of the original hybrids. There are question about their hybrid vigor as they are more prone to clematis wilt. The small-flowered species and hybrids tend to have fibrous roots, while spaghetti or lace-like and somewhat fleshy roots easily identify the large-flowered hybrids.

Raised in New Zealand, *Clematis* 'Prince Charles' is a very prolific flowerer. Flowers which are a beautiful mauvish-blue and semi-nodding are borne from mid-summer to autumn. A compact plant prone to mildew.

Small-flowered species and hybrids

In the order of flowering seasons the small-flowered species and hybrids can be grouped into early and late flowerers.

Early flowering groups

These clematis flower on old wood made during the previous year or years. They should not be pruned, except for general tidying up.

Mid-winter onward

The evergreens, including *Clematis armandii*, *C. cirrhosa*, *C. balearica*, and their hybrids.

Early spring onward

The alpina and its hybrids, including *Clematis alpina* 'Ruby,' *C. alpina* 'Helsingborg;' the macropetala and its hybrids, for example, *Clematis macropetala*, 'Maidwell Hall,' *C. macropetala* 'Rosy O'Grady.'

Late spring to early summer onward

Montana and its hybrids, including *Clematis montana*, *Clematis montana* 'Freda,' *C. montana* 'Marjorie,' *C. montana* 'Broughton Star.'

Late-flowering groups

These clematis flower on new wood made during the current year of growth. They should be pruned hard.

Mid-summer onward

Viticella species and its hybrids, including *Clematis viticella, C. viticella* 'Etoile Violette,' *C. viticella* 'Minuet,' *C. viticella* 'Kermesina.'

Mid-summer to autumn

Tangutica species and its hybrids (yellow clematis), including *Clematis tangutica, C. tangutica* 'Helios,' *C. tangutica* 'Bill Mackenzie,' *C. tangutica* 'Aureolin.'

Late summer onward

Texensis species and its hybrids, including *Clematis texensis* 'Etoile Rose,' *C. texensis* 'Princess Diana,' *C. texensis* 'Gravetye Beauty.'

Large-flowered hybrids

These clematis are all cultivated varieties and can also be grouped into early and late according to their flowering times

**Early
(usually mid-spring to early summer)**

Flowers are produced on old wood made during the previous year or years and do not need regular annual pruning except for thinning out or removal of dead or weak stems. If pruned hard there will be no flowers on plants, including *Clematis* 'Miss Bateman,' *C.* 'Nelly Moser,' *C.* 'Guernsey Cream.' Some of these early-flowering large-flowered hybrids that flower on old wood may also flower again in late summer or early autumn, including *C.* 'Nelly Moser,' *C.* 'Guernsey Cream,' *C.*

'Asao.' Similarly, the large-flowered clematis that bear double flowers may produce single flowers later in the season on growths made during the current year. These include *C.* 'Belle of Woking,' *C.* 'Vyvyan Pennel,' *C.* 'Proteus.'

**Late
(usually mid-summer to early autumn)**

Flowers are produced on new wood made during the current year of growth. These late, large-flowered clematis need severe pruning annually between late winter and early spring to give a good account of themselves. Examples are *Clematis* 'Perle d'Azur,' *C.* ' Hagley Hybrid,' *C.* 'Comtesse de Bouchaud,' and *C.* 'Prince Charles.'

Note that a number of large-flowered clematis can be in flower continuously throughout the summer months.

Nonclimbing herbaceous and semi-herbaceous clematis

Treat these like other herbaceous perennials: some are clump-forming, while others have a tendency to grow tall and should be given adequate supports, although they look good when grown through other shrubs or small trees. Flowers are borne on new growths. They should be pruned hard (see page 34).

An elegant double cultivar, *Clematis* 'Vyvyan Pennel' needs time to settle down, but will do well with care.

Early summer to autumn

Clematis integrifolia, C. integrifolia 'Rosea,' *C. recta, C. heraclefolia, C.* 'Durandii,' *C. jouiniana* 'Praecox.'

Alpine and rock garden clematis

Finally, there are some clematis that make excellent ground-hugging plants and can be grown in a rock or alpine garden. These clematis are relative newcomers on the scene and are mostly from New Zealand. In terms of hybridization their introduction has opened up a number of possibilities. Examples include *Clematis marmoraria, C.* 'Joe' (formerly known as *C. cartmanii* 'Joe'), *C. australis,* and *C.* 'Lunar Lass.'

Naming Procedures

There are at least 600 cultivars of clematis listed in different nursery catalogues and some of their names cause great confusion to the gardener. Even some species are referred to by different names in different parts of the world. The whole purpose of allocating a correct name to a plant is to enable plant specialists and gardeners to know its exact identity irrespective of the part of the world they live in or the language they speak. In recent years, botanists have been very busy, too, changing the old names of some plants. This is indeed necessary, even though gardeners may find it very annoying and frustrating. As recently as 1996, the Royal Horticultural Society (RHS) was appointed by the International Society for Horticultural Science as the international authority for clematis registration and nomenclature. Therefore, errors and confusions about the names of clematis will be sorted out in the end. The Royal Horticultural Society plans to publish the International Clematis Register in the year 2000, and thereafter issue annual supplements. Registration of new cultivars is voluntary and the hybridizers can go a long way in helping the gardener by registering the correct name of the variety with the Clematis Registration Authority.

There are many other problems which need our attention too. Of the large number of hybrids (cultivars) available for sale, not all of them seem to have undergone a proper trial program to establish their quality and worthiness as garden plants. The RHS and the British Clematis Society are conducting long-overdue trial programs on certain groups and individual hybrids of clematis. Furthermore, there are a number of clematis hybrids which have no distinguishing features to separate one from the other. Another problem is the re-introduction of some old hybrids under new names; some nursery catalogues claim these plants are "new." Not all gardeners insist on exacting standards and information. However, it is highly desirable if that efforts are made by nursery growers to supply gardeners with good quality, correctly named plants, accompanied by basic details, such as whether a clematis is a species or hybrid, a climber or herbaceous plant, in addition to the recommended planting aspect, hardiness, height, pruning requirements, and flowering season.

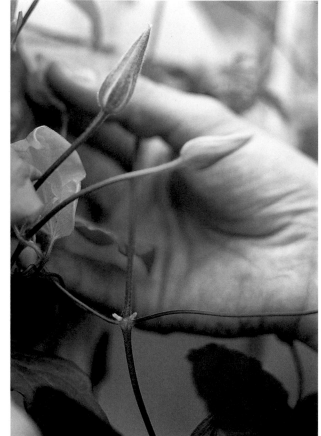

Right: There are no tendrils to help clematis with their climbing habit. Instead the leafstalks or petioles become specially modified to wrap around convenient supports.

Opposite: *Clematis* **'Niobe' is a compact plant with handsome well-shaped flowers. The buds gradually unfurl to display the crushed red velvety tepals.**

Morphology

The genus *Clematis* shares a number of structural characteristics with some other widely grown and much-loved garden plants, such as anemones, aquilegias, delphiniums, hellebores, and pulsatillas. They all belong to one botanical family of plants called Ranunculaceae. However, *Clematis* is the only genus in the family that includes a large number of, mainly woody, climbers. Often gardeners are not aware that the genus also contains some excellent garden-worthy herbaceous or sub-shrubby plants, which deserve to be much more widely grown in our garden borders.

Above and left: The main stem carries the leaves at special points known as nodes or leaf joints. The length of the stem between two consecutive nodes is known as an internode. Note the angles between the main stem and the leaf joints. These are called axils. New buds develop in the axils and grow into new shoots bearing leaves or flowers.

Climbing clematis, in common with many other genera of climbers, have developed modified structures suited to their climbing habits. The petioles or leafstalks of clematis have become modified to twine or wrap around any convenient support and enable them to succeed with their upwardly mobile habit. The flowers of clematis differ from many other flowers in that they have no distinct sepals and petals. In a large majority of flowering plants there are four whorls in each flower, namely **calyx** (sepals), **corolla** (petals), **androecium** (stamens), and **gynoecium** (pistils composed of ovaries, styles, and stigmas). The calyx and corolla are the two outermost whorls of the flower while the androecium and gynoecium are the male and female reproductive or sexual parts, respectively. The sepals of most flowers are green, while the petals boast many different colors. In the case of clematis flowers, there are no true petals. Instead the sepals have become brightly colored to take on the function of petals and are

referred to as being petaloid. The flowers of magnolias, for example, have no true petals either. To distinguish the petaloid sepals from the true petals of many other flowers in the plant world, the term **tepals** is often employed.

The flowers of clematis also show a tremendous diversity in shape, size, form, color, and number of tepals (petaloid sepals). Almost all of them share the common feature of numerous pistils surrounded by an abundance of colorful stamens. Flowers may appear singly or in clusters. They may be hanging, nodding, or appear as open-faced blooms. They may even be beautifully urn-shaped or tulip-like. The number of tepals may be four or more. The color of the flower normally develops as the bud unfurls, and in

Left: Leaves of clematis may be simple (bottom picture) or compound (top picture). Shapes vary from large heart-shaped ones (bottom picture) to finely divided ones. The leaf margins may be smooth or toothed (middle picture).

Right: Note the central boss of creamy-yellow stamens and the feathery looking white stigmas surrounded by the stamens.

the absence of adequate sunlight or if the weather is not warm enough, the tepals may open green. As the flower ages, color will develop. Even the foliage exhibits enormous variations. Some clematis are evergreen, while most are deciduous. Leaves may be simple or compound. The young leaves and shoots may be hairy or smooth (glabrous). Not all clematis leaves are simply green: some may be fresh sea green or bluish green (glaucous), while others may be golden green or even glossy.

A number of clematis carry beautiful seed heads, which are composed of numerous single seeded fruit called "achene." The feathery, persistent styles, also known as tails, of these achenes facilitate seed dispersal.

Cultivating Clematis

Choosing a Clematis

With so many species and hybrids (cultivars) of clematis on sale, gardeners are spoiled for choice. How does a gardener choose a clematis? There is an astonishingly vast array of colors and forms, ranging from the whites, reds, blues, purples, and pinks of the small- and large-flowered hybrids to the small yellow species from Asia. The tendency of course is to fall in love with a clematis in full bloom because of its color or shape and rush to purchase that plant. However, it is a good idea to take some time to consider the following points and gather vital information about the plant before making the actual purchase:

- Is the clematis for garden or container culture?
- What is the planned planting position in the garden: north, south, east, west, exposed or sheltered?
- What space is available for the growth of the plant.
- What type of support will be provided for a climber: natural (tree, shrub, climber, or low-growing perennials); artificial (fence, trellis attached to a wall, or free-standing pergola, arch, obleisk, tripod of rustic poles or canes)?
- Is the plant a species or hybrid?
- Is it a climber or is it herbaceous or a sub-shrub?
- Is the plant evergreen or deciduous?
- Is it hardy or tender?
- Is the growth habit compact or vigorous ?
- What are the ultimate height and spread?
- What is the flowering time?
- What is the flower size (large or small, single or double), and the flower shape and color?
- Does the plant flower on old wood (the previous year's growth) or on new wood (the current year's growth)?
- What are the pruning requirements?

Helpful Hints

If the plant is for a container, make sure it is a compact variety. Not all clematis are suitable for long-term container culture.

Having decided on a particular species or a hybrid, it pays to buy a quality plant from a reputable specialist clematis nursery or a garden center. Of course, it is possible to come across a good plant in a market stall or at a plant sale. Early to mid-spring or early autumn are good times to buy plants. Do buy a healthy, strong-growing plant, even if it is a bit more expensive than the one in the supermarket!

Clematis "liners"

Clematis plants are sometimes sold as "liners" and are inexpensive. In the nursery trade liners are young plants in their first pots. These are not ready for planting out in the garden or in large containers. It is necessary to pot them on and grow them with care for at least another 12 to 18 months before planting them permanently in their allocated space.

Mail-order clematis

If you are buying the plants through a mail-order specialist, it is advisable to do so from a well-known and reputable nursery. Most specialist nurseries produce illustrated catalogues with sufficient information on each plant offered for

---

The Final Choice

Healthy plant
- Mature and well-established in a good-sized pot.
- Two or three good, strong vines or stems.
- Healthy green leaves.
- Not too potbound.
- No roots on the surface of the compost.
- No sign of insect pests.
- No mildew (see page 69).

Unhealthy Plant
- Too young and weak in a very small pot.
- A single, weak vine or stem.
- Withered and brown leaves.
- Severely potbound.
- Roots on the surface of the compost.
- Infested with greenflies, whiteflies, and any other insect pest.
- Stems and leaves show signs of mildew.

Helpful hints

Look for strong healthy basal stems. Well-branched, strong two- or three-stemmed, healthy and bushy plants on short or medium canes or supports are a better buy than single-stemmed, unbranched tall plants on long supports, even if they are in flower.

sale. It is well worth purchasing a catalogue to help choose the plants you want, bearing in mind the following points:

- Evergreen clematis require warm sheltered positions in a garden to grow and flower well.
- Brightly colored flowers—pink, white, or light blue—show up better in shady parts of the garden, as opposed to deep, dark-colored flowers.
- Pale-colored flowers tend to fade in areas of the garden exposed to bright sunshine for most of the day.

- Most clematis require a moist cool root run and therefore, sunny sites will demand regular water supply throughout the growing season.
- Not all clematis can cope with harsh wind or extremely low temperatures.
- Not all clematis are suitable for growing in containers over a long period of time.

Above right: Look for well grown plants in containers. Note the strong growing stems—two or three stems are preferable to a single stem.

Right: Young plant with a single but healthy strong stem.

Left: A very young clematis in its first pot. This plant is not yet ready for planting out in the garden.

Planting Clematis

Although clematis can be bought and planted all the year round because they are container-grown, it makes sense to plant when the soil is not frozen or very wet. Ideal times are early to mid-autumn and late winter to mid-spring.

Autumn planting of clematis is to be highly recommended, with the exception of some tender varieties, such as *Clematis armandii, C. cirrhosa, C. florida,* and *C forsteri* types. During early to mid-autumn the upper layers of the soil are warm and moist and, therefore, very hospitable to a new clematis. Autumn planting will also enable the roots of the clematis to grow into the soil quickly and establish a good root system before the winter arrives and the soil gets colder. Furthermore, since the autumn rains keep the soil moist, regular watering will not be essential. Should the autumn turn out to be dry, however, then watering the newly planted clematis is vital.

Late winter to midspring planting is the next best time to plant all clematis, and the tender varieties in particular. From mid to late spring onward the upper layers of the soil begin to get warmer after the winter. Unless the spring is a wet one, newly planted clematis must not be expected to settle down and grow well without regular watering. Spring planting of the tender varieties will help the plants to get established reasonably well and also allow time for the wood to get ripened by the summer sunshine before winter arrives.

Summer planting of clematis can be undertaken provided every care is taken to keep the plant well-watered throughout the season. Remember most newly planted clematis, and even very well-established ones, need moisture (a cool root run) to grow and flower well.

Winter planting of clematis is also possible but avoid frozen, inhospitable soil. There really is no major advantage in undertaking the job of planting a clematis during the height of winter. Instead, be an armchair clematis hunter, study all the available nursery catalogues and decide on your clematis purchase. A word of caution—not all colors of flowers shown in the illustrations in the catalogues are absolutely correct, especially the blues. Therefore, summer is a good time to visit gardens and plant nurseries that specialize in growing clematis, to see the clematis in flower, and place the order for your chosen plants.

Coarse sand (top), horticultural grit (center), and organic matter (bottom) —compost, peat, or peat-based substitutes—are essential ingredients to condition and enrich the soil before planting a clematis.

Planting sequence:

Top: A hole is dug and prepared with grit ready to receive the plant.

Center: The prepared planting hole is enriched with compost.

Bottom: It is important to hold the root ball carefully and lower it into the prepared hole. Do not remove the canes which support the plant while planting.

Planting in the Garden

An old British saying has it "a Guinea [dollar] for the plant and two for the hole." It may be an old-fashioned maxim but it holds true even in these modern times. It pays to take time and prepare the planting site well. Not all gardeners are blessed with exceptionally fertile, easy-to-work loamy soil. If the soil is not in good condition, preparation before planting a clematis will pay handsome dividends later on.

Soil conditioning

Well-rotted farmyard or horse manure, garden compost, leaf mold, or spent mushroom compost make excellent materials for improving and enriching the soil. If these materials are not readily available, good quality potting compost is a good alternative. If the soil is very heavy clay, the addition of coarse grit, available in garden centers, is to be recommended. If the soil is very sandy and does not hold moisture, it is important to add as much humus (organic matter) as possible before planting clematis. Clematis thrive on good supplies of balanced food and moisture. Once the soil is in good condition planting a clematis is relatively easy.

Soil pH

Contrary to the belief that clematis requires limey or alkaline soil, it will grow satisfactorily on neutral to acid soil. However, the addition of lime to acid soil is advisable for best results

Easy Steps to Planting

Dig a large hole at least twice the size of the pot in which the plant is growing and half as deep again. A good wide and deep hole of at least 1½ x 1½ ft (45 x 45 cm) is essential to accommodate not only the entire root-ball comfortably but also some organic matter.

Loosen the base and side of the hole with a garden fork, particularly if the soil is very compact.

Place some well-rotted manure, leaf mold, or compost, then some top-soil and peat or peat substitute at the very bottom of the planting hole to a depth of at least 4 in. (10 cm). Placing a sufficient quantity of topsoil and peat substitute on top of the manure or compost at the very bottom of the planting hole will prevent the roots of the plant coming into direct contact with the manure or other rich material and being burnt or damaged. If the soil is heavy clay, place some coarse grit or sharp sand at the bottom of the hole before placing any organic material in it, for added drainage and to prevent water logging.

Immerse the container in which the plant is growing in a bucket of water for approximately 10 to 15 minutes to wet the compost thoroughly and enable the uptake of water by the roots. This is a very important prerequisite for planting because, once planted, the roots will require time to grow into the surrounding soil and absorb enough water to distribute to the rest of the plant.

Ease the cane-supported plant with its rootball very carefully out of the container and loosen the roots at the base very gently to facilitate a quick

growth of the roots into the surrounding soil. It is important not to meddle too much with the roots or the rootball.

Place the rootball in the prepared planting hole and ensure that its surface is at least 2¼ in. (6 cm) below the rim of the hole. This will help the plant to develop a healthy basal root crown of buds below the actual soil level. Most of these buds will remain inactive or dormant, until such time as they are called upon to spring into action, should the top growths become accidentally damaged or lost in cultivation or, the plant, notably a large-flowered cultivar, is struck down by clematis wilt. Species clematis do not succumb to wilt, but deep planting is to be very strongly recommended for large-flowered cultivars, just in case!

When the plant is in position fill the area around the rootball with equal parts of good soil and potting compost,

Planting sequence continued.

Right: It is important to firm the plant in position, placing a thick layer of mulch immediately after planting.

Center: Once the clematis is in position, water it thoroughly.

Bottom: Ensure the cane supporting the newly planted clematis is secured carefully to the permanent support. This will prevent wind rocking, help the plant grow away, and form a framework.

Helpful Hints

Do not prune *C. armandii* and its hybrids or other tender evergreen clematis. *C. alpina, C. macropetala,* and *C. montana* and their hybrids will also grow away happily without being pruned, provided the plants are strong and healthy.

Keep a watchful eye on newly planted clematis. If it is planted during spring, slugs and snails will have a feast on the emerging young new growths. Greenflies, too, could be a problem and must be controlled. The secret of success with clematis lies in careful planting and aftercare to ensure that the plant establishes itself quickly and firmly in its new home.

mixed with at least a handful of bone meal or the recommended amount of any general-purpose fertilizer. Do not be over-generous with the fertilizer and always follow the instructions given on the packets or containers.

Now firm the soil and compost mixture around the rootball gently with hands and fist. Place some more of the organic matter used at the bottom of the planting hole around the base of the plant and, away from the stems or vines, making a sort of a mound. This procedure will serve as good mulch and prevent excessive loss of moisture.

It is desirable to plant a low-growing perennial or a shrub reasonably close to the site where the clematis has been planted. This will provide a certain amount of shade for the root system of the clematis. A mound of small-sized gravel could be a suitable alternative to a plant if aesthetics is not a major item on the agenda of the gardener. Do not use slates, slabs, or tiles to shade the clematis roots as these shelter slugs, snails and woodlice.

Attach a permanent label to the plant, with the name of the clematis clearly written and the date of planting.

The cane that came as a support with the plant should be left intact or, if not satisfactory, can be replaced with a stronger cane. The support is necessary for the leafstalks to wrap around and grow away into its host plant, such as a free-standing or wall-supported shrub, or onto an artificial support, such as a trellis on a wall (see page 38). It will also serve to prevent wind rock of the stems which will damage the roots.

Once the planting procedures have been taken care of, the next most vital step is to water the plant well. Give at least 1 gallon (4.5 liters) of water per plant. Regular watering is essential subsequently. If no rain falls within two or three days after the initial watering, repeat the procedure bearing in mind that watering should be related to rainfall. A passing shower may not be adequate, especially if the clematis is planted close to a wall. If summer planting is undertaken, daily watering may be necessary.

Almost all newly planted clematis, particularly the large and small-flowered cultivars regardless of the group they belong to, should be pruned back to at least 12–18 in. (30–45 cm) from the ground the following spring (see page 34). This will encourage plants to throw up new shoots from below the surface of the soil.

Transplanting

Not all clematis can be readily replanted. Species clematis and their cultivated forms with numerous fibrous roots tend not to emerge as convenient rootballs when dug up for transplanting. Also plants such as montanas, established for longer than two or three years, cause problems. However, hybrids of *C. viticella* and other large-flowered varieties lend themselves much more readily to transplanting if initial planting in the wrong site has to be rectified.

The best time to transplant a clematis is late winter, just before the dormant buds burst into growth. Before embarking on the operation of replanting, prune down the stems or the vines to a pair of leaf axil buds (see page 36), within at least 2 ft (60 cm) of the soil level. There is no need to be faint-hearted about this procedure and do not be tempted to leave too many long stems or vines. Severance of some roots during the course of digging up the plant will reduce the size of the root system, which in turn will not be able to transport enough water and other nutrients to the top growths if too many long vines or stems are left on the plant. Re-establishment of the plant in its new site will also be much quicker if the entire framework is smaller. Insert a long bamboo cane in close proximity to the plant and tie in all the vines or stems to the support.

With care, insert the spade into the soil at least 1½ ft (45 cm) away from the base of the plant and dig a circle around it, the aim being to lift an entire rootball. Repeating this operation a few times will enable you to cut all the roots and free the rootball from the surrounding soil. Place the spade under the rootball and gently lift to make sure that all the roots have been cleanly severed. Two spades will be helpful to remove the rootball intact from the site. Get another person to assist, lift the rootball, and place the plant on a heavy-duty polythene sheet or sacking. Keep the rootball covered and moist until it reaches its new site to be replanted.

Adopt the procedure outlined above for planting a new clematis and make sure the planting hole is wide and deep enough to receive the rootball with the shortened stems. Once again it is necessary to plant it at least 2¼ in. (6 cm) deeper than the previous soil level. Untie the stems from the temporary cane support and tie them to the new permanent support or host plant through which the clematis is to grow.

Helpful Hints
If the clematis is evergreen, the best time to transplant is late spring or early autumn. Spray the foliage with water at regular intervals after transplanting to reduce evaporation. Do not attempt to transplant if the plant is in flower. Wait until the period of flowering is over.

Planting in Containers

If containers are the name of the game, especially where no garden space is available, then it pays to take the time and trouble to choose and plant the containers well. Good results can be obtained from growing suitable clematis in containers provided the gardener is prepared to allocate time and care to planting, pruning, training, watering, feeding, and cultivating. The latter includes removal of the top 3 in. (7.5 cm) of compost each year during early spring and top dressing with fresh compost.

Invest in good quality large containers, measuring at least 1½ x 1½ ft (45 x 45 cm), for long-term culture. The larger the container the better for satisfactory performance by the plant. Even then, from my experience of growing clematis in containers, with the exception of very compact plants, such as C. 'Fujimusume' or C. 'Pink Fantasy' and some New Zealand species and hybrids, no clematis should remain in a container after two or three years of growth. Experienced clematarians shy away from long-term pot culture because they know that clematis, especially the large-flowered cultivars, need a good deep root run and no container can possibly give the space these plants require over a long period of time. Many clematis plants may carry labels "Suitable for containers," but be prudent in making your choice.

Although terra-cotta pots make very handsome containers for growing clematis, they do not always afford maximum protection to the plants against heat in the summer and frost in the winter, unless of course they are frost-proof. Oak barrels and other wooden containers, as well as containers made out of stone or concrete, are ideal for growing clematis. Large plastic containers, especially those that imitate terra-cotta pots, are usually not happy with fluctuating temperatures in summer and winter. Nevertheless, by placing these pots with plants in semi-shady or shady places in summer and in sheltered areas in winter, losses can be kept to a minimum. Where possible, clematis planted in large plastic pots can be placed inside large compost-filled containers made of wood, stone or even terra cotta—this operation will enable the gardener to achieve an aesthetically pleasing presentation

as well as move the plant with ease to site it elsewhere, or take it out of the pot altogether, either for repotting or planting out in the garden. In the final analysis, growing clematis in containers should be fun and should never become a major chore or consume all your free time.

The first and most important step in container culture of clematis is to site the empty container in its allocated place first, because once it is filled with compost, planted and well-watered it would be difficult to move in a hurry. A mixture of soil-based and soil-free compost is ideal for container culture. In the garden, roots will work their way through a large volume of soil over a wide area in search of water and nutrients. Plants growing in containers are denied this luxury and, therefore, a well-balanced good potting compost is essential.

Two parts of compost, mixed with one part of peat or peat substitute, is recommended. Whatever compost is used, it is essential to ensure good drainage and at the same time encourage moisture retention. No clematis likes its feet in water!

Above: A well-planted pot of Clematis 'Arctic Queen.' The aim should always be to achieve a very full effect by training the stems right from the start and encouraging a good display of buds and flowers.

Opposite: A novel way of growing Clematis 'Sunset' and C. 'Silver Moon' in a hanging basket. Regular watering and feeding throughout the growing period is essential.

Helpful Hints
Always choose wide-mouthed and wide-based containers to facilitate repotting and prevent the pot from toppling over easily .

Left: *Clematis* **'Blue Angel' is an ideal plant for container growing, but not for long-term pot culture. The tepals of the medium-sized powder blue flowers with crinkled edges boast a delicate texture. The plant is a strong grower and care should be taken to tie in all the shoots carefully to the supporting canes.**

Right: Though *Clematis* **'Durandii' is a herbaceous plant it can be grown successfully in a container. The leaves have no suitable modifications to wrap around the supporting canes and therefore regular training and tying in of the shoots will be essential. Suited for short-term pot culture only.**

To aid drainage, raise the container off the ground by placing custom-made pot stands or half-bricks under it.

Garden soil should not be used in containers because it will become compacted and interfere with drainage. Furthermore, its level of nutrients may be inadequate. It is also likely to contain diseases and pests, especially the vine weevil larvae, which are extremely difficult to control.

Before filling the container with compost, place a layer of small stones, pebbles, or even coarse grit over the drainage holes to prevent the holes being blocked by the compost. A 3 in. (7.5 cm) layer of well-rotted farmyard manure, horse manure, or leaf mold may be placed on top of the stones, pebbles, or grit.

Now fill the remaining space in the container with the compost, leaving at least 2 in. (5 cm) space below the rim of the container to facilitate watering. Firm the compost.

Supporting and Training

Just as a clematis growing in the open garden requires natural or artificial support, container-grown plants also need some support. The type of support will be dictated by the siting of the container. If the aim is to let the plant in the container grow through a wall shrub or a climbing rose, then simply insert a long bamboo cane into the compost, at an angle between the container and the wall or a branch of the wall shrub. As the stems begin to grow these may be tied to the cane support and allowed to take off into the host plant. If the container is sited on a patio, balcony or court-yard, then a suitable support must be given to the plant. There are a great variety of elegant supports on sale and choice will depend on the gardener's personal taste and purse. The support must be securely placed in the container and the stems should be trained onto it. Take every care to prevent or limit wind rock which will cause root damage.

It pays to take some time to train and tie the stems to the support and create an elegant framework from bottom upwards. The ultimate aim should be to produce a bushy plant and not a mass of entangled foliage and flowers at the top of the support. Make use of twine, thin string or any other suitable plant ties to help you achieve a stylishly grown plant in the container. Do not be too worried if some new shoots break accidentally during the course of training and tying—remember for every single broken shoot there will be two new shoots which will break from the leaf axils.

Procedures for planting the clematis in a large container are the same as those for planting clematis in the open garden. Scoop out enough compost in the center of the container to accommodate the plant, after it has been immersed in a bucket of water for about 15 minutes. Remember to plant it at least 2¼ in. (6 cm) deeper than it was in the original pot. Insert a slow-release fertilizer plug, following the recommendations given for its application, into the compost and water well. Plant either a few annuals or a not so vigorous low-growing perennial at the base of the clematis to furnish some shade and prevent excessive loss of moisture. Alternatively, place a layer of gravel or small pebbles on the surface of the compost.

An elegant and deep container is here used to allow *Clematis* 'Elsa Spath' to cascade down the sides. This plant is suitable for growing in containers.

Pinching Out

In fact, it is customary to create a bushy plant by a process of pinching out (the removal of the growing tip of a shoot or a stem with fingernails once each stem has produced two or three nodes). Stop pinching out at least six weeks before the flowering time to allow the plant to develop buds and flower. If growing under glass for exhibiting (see page 118), adjust the time for starting to pinch out growing tips—the earlier the better but do not pinch out more than once. With a little bit of experience you will, of course, master the art of pinching out to make the plant bushy, without necessarily sacrificing the buds and flowers. Experimentation without fear should be the motto.

Pinching out the tip of a growing shoot will help create a fine bushy plant. The photograph shows how to pinch out that part of the growing shoot above a nodal point. Note how the leaf stalks have twined round the cane, which acts as a support (see pp. 16–18).

Aftercare

The garden

During the growing season, from early spring onward, every care must be taken to water and feed all the clematis be they in the open ground or in containers. Clematis are gross feeders and drinkers, and their performance throughout the growing season is dictated by the care they receive. Often gardeners tend to forget that early to mid or late spring may very well be dry and the plants will need water. As soon as new shoots begin to burst from the axillary buds, the time has arrived for showering attention on the plants.

Mulch the plants with well-rotted manure, compost, or any other suitable organic material—be generous with the mulch and, if using manure, try and keep it well away from the stems and emerging young shoots and leaves to prevent any accidental burning and damage.

Sprinkle a handful of bone meal and the recommended dosage of a general-purpose fertilizer on the mulch and fork it in.

Water the plants copiously and gently so that the mulch does not wash away; after that regular watering is important. How often and how much will depend on the amount of rainfall.

As plants grow away actively, use a general-purpose liquid fertilizer; from my experience it is more than adequate to feed once a week following the instructions given on the fertilizer container. Foliar feeding will be beneficial to the leaves. Around mid-spring, replace the general purpose liquid feed with high-potash tomato feed to encourage flowering.

Discontinue feeding once the well-formed plump buds are just about to flower; this will prolong the flowering period. If the plants are fed right through without a break in feeding all the buds will open in quick succession and in a very short period of time.

Helpful Hints

If the late winter to early spring flowering evergreen clematis have been well-fed and nourished during their growing season they will flower very well. If necessary, a light liquid feed may be given to the plants just as the plants show signs of bud formation. Some evergreen clematis (such as *C. cirrhosa* and their hybrids) may go into a period of dormancy during summer. Keep these plants just moist and do not feed. Commence watering and feeding as they wake up from their dormancy.

Recommence the feeding program soon after the flowering period is over. This will help to invigorate the plants and even aid the formation of another small crop of buds and flowers.

Discontinue feeding by early autumn to enable the plants, including the evergreen types, to get ready for their winter rest.

In containers

The same program of feeding clematis in the garden should be applied to clematis growing in containers. If slow-release fertilizer is already incorporated into the compost, be careful not to overfeed using other fertilizers. An alternative to slow-release fertilizer is a general-purpose liquid feed. It will also serve as a good foliar feed. The important thing is not to rely solely on the fertilizer available in the compost of a newly planted container because the amount is limited and is usually exhausted after approximately four to six weeks of growth by plants. More routine watering will be necessary than in open ground because compost tends to dry out much more quickly in containers. The speed with which the compost becomes dry depends on the temperature—during high summer it may be necessary to water the containers twice a day, morning and evening. A passing shower of rain will not wet the compost thoroughly. Adopt a common-sense approach to feeding and watering the containers of clematis throughout the growing and flowering season and derive weeks and months of pleasure from your clematis. Remember to tie in the new growths to the support.

Helpful Hint
Make sure that the compost is moist before watering in the liquid feed to avoid any damage to the roots of the plant.

Caring for container-grown plants during winter

When winter arrives, clematis in containers cannot be expected to fend for themselves. Containers which can be moved should be given shelter in a well-lit place, such as a garage, shed, cold glasshouse, or even a porch. If none of these is available, stand the containers against a warm house or garden wall, or among evergreen shrubs. If the containers are very large and cannot be moved, then follow the procedures set out below:

If the plants have made excessive top growth during summer, prune away the top one-third of stems and tie in the remaining growths to the supports—I use strong green garden twine. The aim is to minimize wind rock and damage to the roots and stems. If the plants flower on old wood there will be a small loss of flowers.

Mulch the plants with peat, compost, or leaf mold to protect the root system.

Incorporate a small handful of slow-release fertilizer, such as bone meal, into the mulch and water it in thoroughly.

If the plants are tender varieties, use horticultural fleece to guard against extremely low temperatures. Two or three layers of fleece wrapped around the plant with the ends held together securely by clothespins or tied with a piece of twine will act as a winter blanket.

Visit the plants at regular intervals and keep the compost moist but not very wet.

Remove the protective covering during late winter or early spring to prune the plants, then replace it until the return of favorable weather. However, overnight protection must be given until fear of late frosts is over.

Helpful Hints
Clematis in containers in the open garden do not enjoy severely wet winters or very low temperatures (below 14°F or 10°C) over a long period of time. Hardy clematis will survive if no protection is given but the flowering potential will be greatly reduced.

Top dressing

Each spring remove the top 3 in. (7.5 cm) of compost carefully with your hands from the container and replace it with a combination of two parts compost and one part peat or peat substitute, as used originally for the planting of the clematis. Check that the plant support is secure. Water and feed as described above.

Repotting

In spite of all the advice given about growing clematis in containers, I strongly believe many are not suited to long-term pot culture. The bootlace roots of large-flowered varieties, including the compact ones often recommended as "suitable for containers," are not able to cope with the restricted spaces and perform well year after year. Regular feeding and watering, of course, help the plants to grow and flower well for two or three seasons. Therefore, it is advisable to give the plants new homes in the open garden after that. If there is no garden or room in the garden, follow my example and plant them in borrowed spaces of a neighbor's or friend's garden. Start fresh with new plants in the old containers.

However, if you must repot it is not a problem provided the pot and the plant are not too large. Late winter or early spring (pruning time in the clematis calendar) is the best time to repot. Ease the rootball gently out of the pot—the drier the compost the easier the job is—and move the plant to a larger pot filled with fresh potting compost. Water the plant and compost thoroughly.

If the container is very large, then you must take the precaution of laying it on its side before easing the rootball out. If necessary, slide a long-bladed knife between the compost and pot to loosen the rootball. A second pair of hands is desirable in carrying out what is a laborious task. If the circum-

ferance of the pot is not very wide, the rootball may be too big to be eased out. In this situation, you may have to use an implement, such as a strong carving knife, to cut the outer 2–3 in. (5–7.5 cm) of the rootball in situ before attempting to remove it from the container. Having successfully completed this part of the operation, you may have to reduce the size of the rootball by some judicious root pruning, that is, by cutting off 2–3 in. (5–7.5 cm) of roots, or even more, from the outer edges. Take a well-earned break from the plant and its rootball at this stage, clean out the container, and have a cup of tea. Proceed with repotting, following the steps given for planting in containers. Do remember to plant the clematis at least 2¼ in. (6 cm) deeper than it was originally.

Root pruning and repotting may be daunting tasks to a novice container gardener but rest assured, a clematis with a good root system seldom gives up the ghost! I have been ruthless with my sharp knife: recently I had a battle with the rootball of a large-flowered clematis growing in a pot for two years. After easing out the rootball, I pruned back the stems by more than

half and carried out severe root pruning. The plant with its rootball was placed in a heavy-duty black polythene bag with some fresh compost and watered thoroughly; some slug pellets were scattered in, and the clematis was left in the corner of a garden for a few days. New shoots grew away merrily, the plant looked happy and was repotted in the same container—cleaned out thoroughly and filled with fresh potting compost. Next time around the same clematis will be found a place in the open ground—better for the plant and its owner.

Helpful Hints
Do not pull out the plant by its stems, even if they look sturdy. If a cane or canes support the plant, remove them before embarking on repotting to prevent any accidental injuries to yourself or your assistant. Do not indulge in severe pruning if the plant flowers on old wood, although reduction of the stems will be essential even if it means loss of flowers. New roots must grow to support the old stems and the new growths.

Pruning

Nature has its own methods of eliminating superfluous growths to ensure that plants grow healthily, vigorously, and flower well. The reason behind pruning clematis in the garden is primarily to encourage healthy and vigorous growth and secondarily to establish a handsome framework and make the most of the space available in the garden. Many gardeners consider pruning of clematis to be complicated, difficult, and even puzzling. Some are reluctant to tackle this business of pruning for fear they will lose their plants. In reality a large majority of clematis does not need regular pruning at all.

Group 1
Clematis, both evergreen and deciduous, that flower before early summer on old ripened wood, just like many flowering trees and shrubs which flower before early summer, generally do not require any pruning at all. Therefore, a simple rule is: "If your clematis flowers before early summer, do not prune." This means all winter and spring-flowering clematis, including *Clematis cirrhosa*, *C. balearica*, *C. napaulensis*, *C. forsteri*, *C. armandii*, *C. macropetala* and its cultivars, *C. alpina* and its cultivars, and many others, virtually need no pruning and will flower year after year. However, should they

Group 2

Some clematis produce two flushes of flowers; the first appears before early summer on old ripened growths made during the previous year and the second on new growths made in the current year during late summer. Among these are *C.* 'Nelly Moser,' *C.* 'Niobe,' *C.* 'Bee's Jubilee,' *C. florida* and its cultivars, *C.* 'Miss Bateman,' *C.* 'H. F. Young.' These clematis belong to Group 2, as do all the clematis which produce double or semi-double flowers, including *C.* 'Proteus,' *C.* 'Vyvyan Pennel,' *C.* 'Sylvia Denny,' *C.* 'Duchess of Edinburgh,' *C.* 'Louise Rowe,' *C.* 'Royalty,' and *C.* 'Arctic Queen.' Group 2 clematis do not need major pruning but it is a good idea to cut out all dead and weak shoots in

need pruning because they have outgrown their allocated spaces or become overgrown and untidy, a certain amount of tidying up and cutting back can be undertaken immediately after they have finished flowering. This will enable the plants to produce new growths, which will have time to get ripened by the sun during summer and be ready to flower the following spring. For convenience, all clematis which flower before early summer are placed together in Group 1.

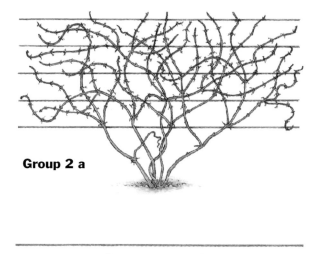

Right: Group 2. Before tidying up the plant (2a). You should avoid large-scale pruning. Thinning out is the aim to achieve a neat framework (2b).

Group 2 a

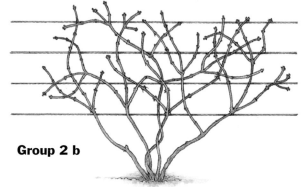

Below: Group 1. Carefully trained to its support, clematis (alpinas, macropetalas, montanas, and evergreen varieties) that flower on old wood (previous year's growths) will make a handsome display of flowers from early spring to early summer. Any tidying up should be carried out immediately after the period of flowering.

Group 2 b

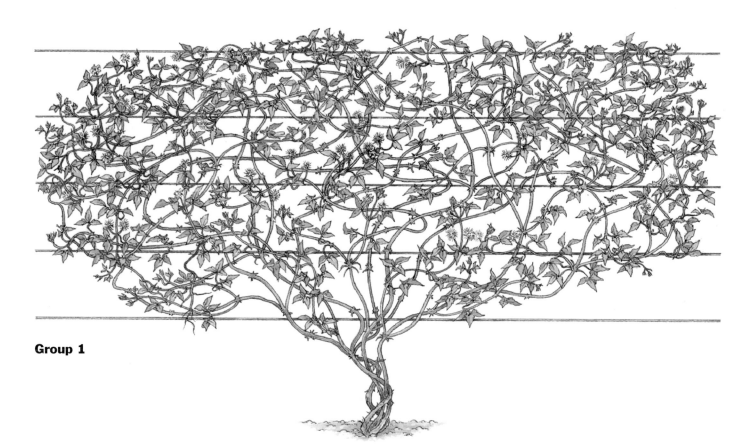

Group 1

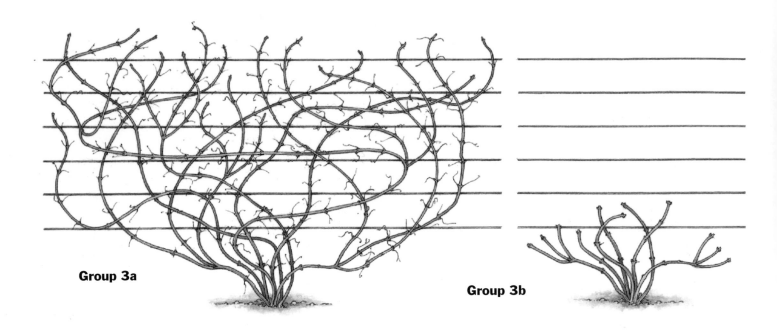

Group 3a

Group 3b

late winter to early spring. This is best achieved by working your way down from the top of each stem until you come across a pair of plump, healthy buds. Prune just above them. The general rule for pruning Group 2 clematis is: "Refrain from wide-scale pruning or there will be no early flowers."

Group 3

Clematis that flower after early summer or those commonly referred to as late-summer flowering species and varieties, need annual pruning during late winter to early spring, or even slightly later depending on how early or late the spring arrives, because they all flower on the current year's growths, including small-flowered viticellas, orientalis, texensis groups and large-flowered plants such as C. 'Comtesse de Bouchaud,' C. 'Gipsy Queen,' C. 'Hagley Hybrid,' C. 'Lady Betty Balfour,' and C. 'Star

of India.' These belong to Group 3 and must be pruned very hard. A quick and easy way to prune these is to start at the base of the stems and work upwards until you meet the first pair of healthy, plump buds. Prune the stems just above the buds and remove all the old growths above the cut. Patience is all that is required here. Harsh as this treatment may sound, the plants will be encouraged to make strong new shoots and produce an abundance of flowers. Spare the pruning shears and you will spoil the growing habits and flowering ability of these clematis! The general rule for pruning Group 3 clematis is: "Prune back all the old stems to the lowest live buds."

Above: Group 3. Clematis ready for pruning during the early spring (3a). Prune back hard and without fear to achieve the result shown in 3b.

Quick Guide to Pruning

Read the plant label to ascertain the group to which the clematis belongs and months of flowering.

Flowering time before early summer (Group 1): do not prune. Any tidying up or removal of some flowered stems should be done immediately after flowering.

Two flushes of flowers, early summer to late summer (Group 2): tidy up and remove some weak and dead wood during late winter or early spring and do

not indulge in large-scale severe cutting back of old or new stems.

Flowering time after mid-summer through to late summer and even early fall (Group 3): cut back all the old stems hard to the lowest live buds. Vigorous plants, such as C. tangutica and its cultivars, need not take up too much of your time. Simply gather all the old growths in your hand and cut right through all the stems at a point about 1 ft (30 cm) from ground level.

Pruning of clematis grown in association with shrubs, trees, roses, conifers, heathers, and other climbers

Clematis grown as companion plants are discussed on page 38. Pruning of these clematis, notably those which belong to Group 3, can be accomplished in two simple steps:

Remove all the top growths of deciduous clematis, which look unsightly after leaf fall, to allow the natural supports to look their best during winter.

Complete the pruning program in early spring. Take care not to undertake any hard pruning if the clematis belong to Groups 1 or 2.

Pruning of plants of unknown identity

There are times when you may not know the name of a plant to ascertain the pruning group to which it belongs. Perhaps you have lost the label, or become the new owner of an old garden with a number of clematis plants without labels. Where the identity of plants is not known, do not rush to prune them, particularly in an old garden. Get a clematis expert or a nursery grower to identify the plants for you. Failing that, allocate a number to each of the plants and observe their flowering pattern and time over a period of twelve months. Keep a record. The pruning guide outlined above will assist you in placing the plants in the appropriate category for pruning. Investing in an illustrated book on clematis to identify your plants is a good idea. If you are unable to find an expert or nursery grower in your area write to a Clematis Society for assistance with identification of your plants.

Care after pruning

Soon after pruning, sprinkle a general purpose granular fertilizer and bone meal or fish, blood, and bone meal, following the dosage recommended by the manufacturers and gently fork it into the soil surface. Cover with a thick layer of compost, well-rotted farmyard manure, horse manure, or any other material which will serve as a suitable mulch and conserve moisture at the roots. It is advisable to use a pair of gloves when handling farmyard manure and fertilizers such as bone meal.

General and useful notes and hints

Clematis are ideally suited to urban and country gardens of all sizes and shapes. There are a wealth of species and hybrids to choose from. If you do not succeed the first time with one plant, try again with another but do not dig up and discard the rootball. Leave a cane in situ to identify the plant. Clematis have been known to disappear for a while and re-appear out of the blue like phoenixes from the ashes, to the surprise and delight of gardeners.

Be patient with clematis and give it a minimum of three growing seasons. With careful planting, watering, and feeding, the aim should be to allow the plant to establish a good strong root system and throw up healthy shoots from beneath the soil.

If pruning causes a problem, visit a specialist nursery during early spring and seek help or consult the experts at a horticultural show. Some specialist clematis nurseries hold open pruning days—you may be lucky enough to have one in your area. Never be afraid of pruning or losing your clematis, even if the plant has only one stem, as long as you can locate a pair of plump buds, just cut above that point and treat yourself to two shoots. If the winter is mild some late summer-flowering clematis may burst into growth much earlier than spring and before the actual annual pruning time. You can cut away these new growths and shorten the old stems without any apprehension. Then work your way down to seek and find a pair of plump buds remaining dormant or inactive on each stem: just cut above the leaf joints and all should be well. Plants know how to cope with the vagaries of the weather.

Start with some easy clematis, such as small-flowered *alpina*, *macropetala*, and *viticella* species and their varieties and graduate to large-flowered hybrids.

There are occasions, especially during late spring and early summer, when suddenly some plump buds and even stems of large-flowered hybrids may simply wither and droop. My observation leads me to believe that sudden changes in humidity, temperature, and even wind may be responsible for the onset of wilt, a fungal disease (see page 69) that causes an unfortunate collapse of flower buds and stems. Should any of your large-flowered clematis be suddenly struck down by wilt, let there be no panic. Simply remove the top growths and burn them—do not throw them on your compost heap. Invariably new shoots will appear from below the soil. From my experience of growing clematis, a few, which are prone to wilt, learn to grow out of it and become strong and healthy plants, behave themselves, and flower beautifully.

Slugs and snails with their rasping tongues may destroy young shoots, so beware of these garden pests as well.

Ways of Growing Clematis

Like most climbing plants in our gardens, clematis demand suitable supports to climb on and show off their blooms. With more and more gardeners becoming very particular about design and elegance in the garden, gone are the days when we planted a clematis against a wall, "crucified" it, and forgot about it. With careful planning and forethought, clematis can be grown in many different ways to add to the elegance and beauty of any garden. There are a number of man-made structures, some especially suited to growing clematis, available on the market, including trellises of all shapes and sizes, pergolas, arches, and obelisks. Imaginative gardeners construct their own structures with rustic poles, bamboo canes, and wood to train and grow their clematis in the garden. While artificial supports have their place in the garden for helping the clematis to attain their vertical growth, we must remember that in the wild they grow in association with other plants. Even a quick glance at the manner in which *Clematis vitalba* makes its way through other plants in any neglected land or hedge will demonstrate the versatility of clematis. William Robinson, famous gardener and author of *The Virgin's Bower* (1912), perfected the art of growing clematis the "natural" way by planting them in the shade of a low tree or shrub and allowing them to grow freely, as in the wild, to achieve many beautiful effects in his garden at Gravetye Manor in West Sussex. Thankfully, more and more gardeners are growing clematis in association with other garden plants. Pairing a clematis with a shrub, tree, conifer, or another climbing plant should be done carefully. Roses are particularly popular supports.

Basic rules for pairing a clematis with a supporting plant

- Consider the growth habits, flowering times, and pruning requirements of the clematis and the supporting plant, prior to embarking on planting a clematis in close proximity to an existing shrub, tree, or other plant, in the garden.
- Do not plant a very vigorous clematis through a less vigorous, garden shrub, tree, rose, or other plant.
- Do not plant a compact clematis through a large shrub or tree.
- Do not plant the clematis and the supporting plant simultaneously. Allow time for the host plant to establish itself first before expecting it to play a supportive role.
- Do not grow an evergreen clematis through a deciduous plant which will require regular pruning.
- Decide whether you want the clematis and the supporting plant to flower at the same time or at different times. If the former, choose a clematis whose flowers will complement those of the supporting plant and vice versa.
- Do not grow a clematis through a hedge which requires regular clipping and maintenance.
- Do not be afraid to rectify any mistakes. With all the planning and care in the world, there are times when the pairing could go wrong.

In the absence of suitable leaf-stalk modifications to wrap around its support, this *Clematis* 'Durandii' has utilized branches of a medium-size tree to hold its stems well and show off its splendid flowers.

Through Trees and Shrubs

When planting a clematis close to a tree or a shrub, take extra care to site it on the side not reached by the midday sun, that is, the area that does not dry up quickly and so remains cool and reasonably moist. It is advisable to find a spot at a distance from the tree or shrub and either train the stems of the clematis along the ground and lead them into the host plant, or train them directly into the branches with the aid of a strong twine. However, I have seen clematis planted very close to the main trunk of a tree thriving in some gardens.

Once you find a suitable place to plant the clematis to grow in association with a tree or a shrub, the most important thing is to take time and enrich the hole with as much organic material as possible. Regular watering and feeding are essential for the healthy growth of the clematis. Should you wish to clothe the main trunk of a tree with a clematis, wrap the required length of chicken wire loosely round the trunk. Lead the stems of the

Early summer flowers are displayed with great charm and elegance by allowing this *Clematis* 'Marie Boisselot' to grow through the branches of a medium-sized tree.

clematis towards the chicken wire, which will enable the plant to climb up and away into the main branches of the supporting tree.

Choose the tree carefully. There are a number of handsome deciduous trees, which look splendid in winter, and it would be a pity to spoil their appearance by growing vigorous clematis, such as montanas, through them. Expansive and well-established trees also have extensive root systems, which will be very difficult for the clematis to compete with. Therefore, it is advisable to leave those trees alone and select a small to medium deciduous tree, such as *Crataegus laevigata* 'Paul Scarlet,' *Malus* 'Golden Hornet,' *Sorbus acuparia* 'Joseph Rock,' *Sorbus cashmiriana*, *Prunus* 'Amanogawa,' *Prunus* x *subhirtella* 'Autumnalis,' *Pyrus salcifolia* 'Pendula,' *Fagus sylvatica* 'Dawyck' (conical to broadly columnar beech), for example.

In my own small urban garden, *Clematis alpina* 'Pamela Jackman' and *C.* 'Nelly Moser' are hosted by *Sorbus* 'Joseph Rock,' planted on the north side of the garden. 'Pamela Jackman' has invaded every upright branch of the tree and comes into flower well before the tree shows any signs of its beautiful foliage. I believe it is an ideal way to grow and admire the hanging, beautifully blue flowers of

this clematis. The manner in which the flowers are displayed also allows me to enjoy the central part of the flower. 'Nelly Moser' is trained on chicken wire wrapped carefully around the single standard stem of *Sorbus*, and she comes into flower a little bit later than 'Pamela Jackman.' Apart from an occasional tidying up of the two clematis, no major pruning job is undertaken. Even the semi-herbaceous *C.* 'Durandii' growing about 3 ft (90 cm) away from *Sorbus* happily invades the tree to show off its blooms later on in the season.

Clematis 'Miss Bateman' enjoys her partnership with hawthorn and manages to show off her flowers well before the hawthorn puts out its spring foliage, while *C. macropetala* 'Markham's Pink' is more than comfortable with the winter-flowering cherry, *Prunus subhirtella* 'Autumnalis.' The late flowers and slightly bronze young leaves of the cherry tree look simply stunning with those of 'Markham's Pink.' The 15-year-old *Fagus sylvatica* 'Dawyck' (Dawyck beech), on the other hand, has happily taken on two strong-growing clematis, *C. ternata*

'Robusta' and *C. tibetana* ssp. *vernayi*. The tree and the stems of the clematis enjoy basking in the midday and evening sunshine, which means that there is no shortage of flowers from these late-flowering clematis. *Clematis tangutica* 'Bill Mackenzie' planted at a distance from a handsome white-barked *Betula utilis* var. *jacquemontii* (Himalayan birch), manages to make its way into the branches of the tree each year, and the yellow, open, bell-shaped flowers transform the tree from late summer onwards. Even without deliberate planning and planting, some clematis manage to seek and find their own partners in trees and shrubs in the garden as they often do in the wild.

An imaginative gardener has numerous ways of partnering a clematis or two with a tree. For example, an old mature *Pyrus salcifolia* 'Pendula' (the weeping pear tree) could offer a magnificent growing surface for the late-flowering *Clematis viticella* 'Polish Spirit' (rich purple flowers), the 'Star of India,' or the 'Gipsy Queen' or, if you prefer an early-flowering clematis, *C. macropetala* 'Maidwell Hall' (rich blue flowers).

Holly trees make excellent supporting partners for a number of clematis that require hard pruning and flower from mid-summer onwards. *Ilex aquifolium* 'Ovata Aurea' has a neat compact habit and the leaves are spineless. It is also a male clone and does not produce berries. Here then is a delightful holly, which can play a perfect host to *C.* 'Comtesse de Bouchaud' (pink flowers) or *C.* 'Madame Julia Correvon' (claret red flowers). Both these clematis need severe pruning, and they will come to no harm if a certain amount of the top growths are removed after late autumn and pruned further down to healthy plump buds during late winter or early spring. Another partnership to be recommended is one between *Ilex* x *altaclerensis* 'Lawsoniana,' a bright and attractive holly with a large splash of golden yellow marking the dark green leaves, and *C. viticella* 'Abundance' (crimson flowers) or *C.* 'Ville de Lyon' (cherry-red flowers). *C.* 'Huldine' (pearl white flowers) would look splendid with the broadly columnar evergreen bay tree, *Laurus nobilis*, which boasts lovely leathery leaves. Fruit trees, such as apple and plum, similarly make excellent plants through which clematis can be trained.

There are many medium to large shrubs which are also excellent host plants for clematis to

Clematis 'Hagley Hybrid' is a popular and widely grown clematis. It is very floriferous over a long period of time if trained on an artificial support. May also be grown through evergreen and deciduous shrubs or as a small mound at ground level. Plant away from full sun to prevent the shell pink color fading.

grow through and make an impact. Plants like *Garrya elliptica*, *Forsythia*, and *Corylus avellana* 'Contorta' have very little to offer the gardener from late spring onward, once their peak time is over. By growing some mid to late-season flowering clematis through those shrubs, a new dimension of color is introduced into areas in the garden which would otherwise be rather dull. *Clematis viticella* 'Alba Lux-

urians' (white flowers with splashes of green) brightens my *Garrya elliptica*, while the shell-pink flowers of 'Hagley Hybrid,' partnered with the corkscrew hazel, elect to sit flat on top of the rather dull leaves of its host plant and win the admiration of my family and visitors to the garden.

One of the major advantages of growing clematis such as 'Ville de Lyon,' 'Hagley Hybrid,' and 'Perle d'Azur' through shrubs lies in the fact that their inevitably bare and leggy stems get well hidden by the foliage of their host plants. *Escallonia* 'Gold Brian' makes a useful and elegant partner for *Clematis* 'Arabella' (rosy purple flowers with a bit of red sheen). 'Arabella' not being equipped with leaf modifications to wrap around its support can be allowed to scramble through the escallonia and the flowers show up very well against the golden foliage. Two years ago, *C.* 'Pink fantasy' managed to find its way into the *escallonia* and, much to my surprise, the combination turned out to be quite elegant. *Viburnum* x *bodnantense* 'Dawn,' a winter-flowering scented shrub planted in the middle of a sunny border in my garden, happily took on the early-flowering *C. alpina* 'Ruby.' The purply pink flowers of 'Ruby' not

only look just perfect with the somewhat bronzy green young leaves of the viburnum but also look vibrant in the sunshine. In the opinion of the author, *Clematis viticella* 'Purpurea Plena' (syn. *C. v.* 'Mary Rose') with its double, smoky mauvish flowers makes no impression when grown on its own. Associated with *Choisya ternata* 'Sundance' it is a different story altogether.

There are endless possibilities for associating clematis, both species and hybrids, with trees and shrubs. Taking on the challenge and the art of working out "who with whom?" could be fun. Let your imagination run riot in the garden. Try growing *C.* 'Cholmondeley' (light blue flowers) through *Ceanothus arboreus* 'Trewithen Blue' an early-flowering large wall shrub with powder-blue flowers—just magnificent!

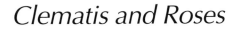

Clematis and Roses

Rosarians and clematarians would agree on one point— roses and clematis are natural companions. It stands to reason, then, to try and grow as many clematis as possible with roses. The growing requirements of both groups of plants are somewhat similar, and if the clematis that belong to Group 3 and require hard pruning are planted in association with roses that require pruning, the whole pruning exercise could be achieved in or around the same time. However, with information on the flowering periods and pruning requirements of clematis and roses accompanied by careful planning, it is possible to achieve some clever and exciting ways to grow clematis with roses.

- Clematis that will flower before the rose comes into flower.
- Clematis that will flower when the rose is flowering.
- Clematis that will flower after the rose has flowered.
- Clematis as ground cover on rose beds.
- Clematis between or near roses, especially if they are grown against a long wall or a fence.

The choice of growing roses and clematis is often dictated by the amount of space available in a garden to accommodate these plants. Growing roses and clematis together will demand time and patience but the amount of time available to spend on leisure activities may be limited. As a result, wise choices will have to be made in the garden with regard to planting and maintenance. Gardening is primarily about relaxation and enjoyment. Passionate clematarians and rosarians deal with their plants somewhat differently, and the following account is mainly aimed at those gardeners who wish to make the most of their time and space in the garden.

Many clematis can be successfully grown through old-fashioned shrub roses, wall-trained climbing roses, ramblers, roses grown on pergolas, arches, pillars, and free-standing poles. The essential requisite is to match the vigor of the clematis with that of the supporting rose plant. No clematis should be allowed to smother and

41

A successful combination: *Clematis* 'Comtesse de Bouchaud' enjoys its company with the rambling rose 'Brenda Colvin.' *Solamun crispum* 'Glasnevin' will carry on flowering into autumn providing much needed color to the clematis/rose partnership after their flowering period is over.

overpower the rose. The aim of a clematis-rose partnership should be to derive maximum pleasure from the flowers individually, and in combination if the flowering times of the two plants coincide. In the latter case, careful matching of colors is necessary. With a bit of experience and, no doubt, by trial and error over a period of time, the ultimate association between these two groups of plants can be achieved.

I have successfully planted an early-flowering and vigorous *Rosa banksiae* 'Lutea' beside a *Clematis montana* var. *rubens*, utilizing a wall nearly 60 ft (20 m) long by 6½ ft (2 m) high in my borrowed rectory garden. Despite the fact that both are vigorous plants, by carefully thinning out the plants immediately after flowering and even removing a portion of the stems during the winter months, albeit at the loss of flowers, a certain sanity and control have been introduced into these plants.

Early-flowering *alpinas* and *macropetalas* make a welcome splash of color ahead of the roses. However, over a period of time they will need to be thinned out or even cut

back if you do not wish your roses to be damaged. Often, we plant certain clematis with the best intentions of grooming and manicuring but time does not allow us to deal with every aspect of growing any plant, let alone clematis. The following clematis, recommended for growing with roses, should not put any gardener under pressure and yet ensure enjoyment in growing the plants with roses.

Large-flowered early summer-flowering cultivars

Clematis 'Lasurstern' (mid-blue), *C.* 'Mrs Cholmondeley' (light lavender blue), *C.* 'Gillian Blades' (white), *C.* 'Jackmanii Alba' (double blue-white), *C.* 'Henryi' (white), *C.* 'Dawn' (pearly pink), *C.* 'Fair Rosamond' (flesh pink with a hint of a pink bar), *C.* 'General Sikorski' (mauve-blue), *C.* 'Comtesse de Bouchaud' (mid-pink), *C.* 'Anna Louise' (violet with red-purple bar), *C.* 'Elsa Späth (mid-blue), *C.* 'Rhapsody'(sapphire blue), *C.* 'Snow Queen' (bluey white).

Viticellas

C. viticella 'Abundance' (deep pink-red), *C. v.* 'Alba Luxurians' (nodding white bell, green tips on early flowers), *C. v.* 'Betty Corning' (pinkish mauve with a hint of scent), *C. v.* 'Etoile Violette' (dark purple), *C. v.* 'Kermesina' (crimson with a white spot at the base of the sepals), *C. v.* 'Little Nell' (creamy white with

mauve-pink margins), *C. v.* 'Madame Julia Correvon (rich red), *C. v.* 'Minuet' (purple-red), and others.

Late-flowering species and small-flowered cultivars

Clematis 'Helios' (yellow), *C.* 'Golden Tiara' (yellow), *C. texensis* 'Etoile Rose' (pale pink with rosy bar), *C. texensis* 'Princess Diana' (vibrant pink), *C.* 'Pagoda' (pale mauve-pink), *C.* x *triternata* 'Rubromarginata' (white with red-purple tips), and many others.

A note on pruning clematis grown with roses

If any of the clematis you choose to plant with roses belong to Group 2, and the rose needs pruning, adopt the same procedure as you would for Group 3 clematis. The early flowers will be lost but there will be a display later in the season.

Popular climbing roses, such as *Rosa* 'Maigold,' *R.* 'New Dawn,' *R.* 'School Girl,' *R.* 'Compassion,' *R.* 'Albertine,' *R.* 'Galway Bay,' *R.* 'Golden Showers,' and *R.* 'Handel' would be excellent plants to grow in combination with clematis. Personal tastes, of course, will dictate the clematis-rose associations. There is a wealth of species and hybrids in both groups of plants from which any gardener can choose what he or she wishes to grow together, but the choice must be made carefully for the best results.

Clematis and Conifers

Many large and medium-sized conifers can be clothed effectively with some strong-growing clematis that flower in abundance. Invariably, many gardeners grow the *montanas* and their varieties on their own and they are usually used to cover an unsightly wall, fence or shed. How delightful it would be to see garlands of *Clematis montana* f. *grandiflora* or var. *rubens* covering the branches of a well-established *macrocarpa* or a *leylandii*. It would be unwise to grow clematis through, or up and over some splendidly shaped and beautiful garden conifers: however, the author has successfully planted a *C.* 'Perle d'Azur' on the north side of a handsome Korean fir, *Abies koreana*. The clematis grows exceptionally well up and over one side of the conifer and the flowers cascade down every summer—a joy to behold. The stems lying on the conifer are lifted off the plant and cut back by about one-third in late autumn each year. This out of season first-stage pruning of the clematis enables the conifer to show off its cones and look well during Christmas time. A number of summer and late-flowering clematis, such as the texensis varieties, *C.* 'Gipsy Queen,' *C. jackmanii* 'Superba,' and others, can be grown over vigorous, prostrate golden conifers. The latter may serve as hiding places for snails, so be careful and keep a watchful eye on them—the young shoots of clematis could very well end up in the jaws of these garden pests.

This white montana merrily works its way through *Cupressus leylandii* to put on a generous display of flowers over a long period.

Clematis as Ground Cover

Although many gardeners tend to grow and display clematis on walls, trellises, and other suitable supports, quite a few varieties can be grown along the ground. Plant the clematis in the usual way and route the stems horizontally. Make "hairpins" from lengths of wire and use these to hold the stems in place on the ground. Some compact varieties, *Clematis* 'Pink Fantasy,' C. 'H.F.Young,' C. 'Niobe,' for example, carefully trained would look splendid—as would some of the *texensis* hybrids, such as 'Gravetye Beauty,' with their tulip-shaped flowers. However, training these painstakingly and ensuring that the new shoots are not attacked by snails, slugs, and other garden pests would be time-consuming. Depending on how much gardening space is available, vigorous varieties, such as *montanas* (early flowering) and *Clematis* x *jouiniana* 'Praecox' (late flowering) could be very successfully grown as ground cover plants and should not demand too much of your time.

Growing and training clematis on man-made supports

Not all gardeners wish to grow their clematis in association with other garden plants. If that is the case, choose the clematis and their man-made supports very carefully. Many clever ways of using a variety of supports for growing clematis can be gleaned by visiting private and public gardens. Some clematis nurseries also have their own display gardens to demonstrate ways and means of growing clematis on supports.

However, structures must be chosen to fit in with your own garden design and planting. Walls are great assets in any garden and can be made full use of for growing clematis but will require suitable structures, such as trellis, square mesh wire or lengths of plastic-coated strong wires to enable the leaf-stalks of clematis to wrap around them and grow away. Fences also make good supports but remember to run vertical and horizontal wires as necessary to help the clematis to clasp and climb. Do not despair if there are no garden walls or fences. Free-standing structures judiciously erected or placed in the garden are suitable alternatives.

Clematis **'Peveril Pearl' trained against a pillar. Pillars make good supports for growing clematis and climbing roses together.**

Walls of clematis

The base of a wall can be very dry because of its foundation, and passing showers of rain seldom reach the area. Therefore, it is important to plant a clematis at least 1–1½ ft (30–45 cm) away from the base of the wall and enrich the planting hole with as much moisture-retentive organic matter as possible. A clematis planted against the wall will need a regular water supply and a heavy mulch to conserve moisture. It is also desirable to plant suitable wall shrubs or other climbers as good neighbors for clematis trained to grow on walls. If the clematis is not evergreen, a wall covered in naked stems of clematis may not be a pleasing sight during long winter months.

Hardwood or plastic trellis comes in different shapes and sizes. Trellis that gives a three-dimensional effect is particularly effective when mounted on walls. Choice of trellis for the wall will be dictated by personal taste of course. It pays to invest in heavy-duty hardwood trellis if wood is preferred to plastic. A word on hanging a trellis on the wall: do not place the trellis flat against the wall. Fix the trellis with the aid of screws on small blocks of wood treated with wood preservative. Allow a space of at least 1 in. (2.5 cm) between the wall and trellis so that there will be room for air circulation, thus preventing mildew; in addition, the stems will be able to clamber up the space behind the support, enabling the leaf stalks to wrap around it and also facilitate the task of tying in the growths, if necessary, with ease.

If the walls need regular painting, opt for free-standing trellis in front of the wall, allowing enough standing room between the wall and the trellis.

If the wall, with suitable support, is used for growing vigorous non-pruning varieties of clematis—*alpina* or *macropetala* and some evergreen types, for example—these plants can become a thicket over a number of years, so it is a good idea to thin out the plants annually once they have established a good framework. Remember to undertake this task of pruning immediately after flowering if they belong to Group 1 (see page 34). Walls and trellis also provide a resting and hiding place for snails. Keep an eye on these unwelcome visitors. If the young shoots are disappearing or stems are withering or wilting it may very well be due to relentless snail and slug activities (see page 68).

Free-standing trellis, obelisks, and other plant supports

Clematis-clad, free-standing supports erected or sited carefully among other garden plants in borders create a vertical dimension and interest in any garden, small or large. Let your imagination run riot and choose good quality and aesthetically pleasing wooden and metal structures to achieve elegance and height in otherwise flat areas of the garden. Large, medium, and small obelisks grouped together with clematis growing on them will lend a focal point in a garden. Choose your clematis wisely. For a list of suitable clematis to festoon free-standing supports see page 121.

Arches and pergolas

A wide range of arches and pergolas are available to the modern gardener. Ideally they should be sited in sunny positions in the garden to support clematis in association with climbing or pillar roses or any other suitable climbers. Plants with pendulous flowers look most effective when grown against pergolas and arches. Where possible, choose plants with scent or aromatic foliage and long or remontant flowering habits. However,

Though a clematis, like this **C.** **'Lasurstern,'** grown against a trellis will grow happily away, it pays to train and tie in the stems to achieve an elegant display of foliage and flowers.

Arches and pergolas also lend themselves to planting clematis with climbing roses or other suitable climbing plants. Try clematis such as 'Perle d'Azur' or 'Madame Julia Correvon' with *Rosa* 'Golden Showers,' which produces flowers continually throughout the summer. The rose also has a moderate fragrance.

If there is unlimited space for gardening and plenty of room for erecting tall, wide arches or long pergolas, there is no reason why the gardener should not indulge in planting quick-growing clematis. However, the pleasure given by a vigorous plant in full flight of flowers on a pergola may very well be diminished when it comes to maintaining the plant, should it become unruly and spill over the path beneath.

A word of caution on planting evergreen clematis to grow up and over pergolas or acrches. If you intend walking under these structures during wet days in autumn and winter, don't forget the menace of rain-drip from the heavy foliage. Of course, the problem does not arise if the pergolas or arches do not lead anywhere in the garden. Having said that, my *Clematis cirrhosa* 'Freckles' occupies a pergola specially built for it close to the gable wall of the house. The plant is sheletered by the wall, the pendulous flowers look superb when they hang down and I can look up into the flowers where all their beauty lies.

Pillars and posts or poles of clematis

Pillars constructed of bricks, blocks, and stones, wooden posts and rustic poles make good solid supports for clematis. Wrap chicken wire, with a mesh size of 2 in. (5 cm), around these supports to provide a surface for the leaf stalks of clematis to twine around and climb.

Festoons of clematis

Space permitting, a row of posts erected in a semicircle, circle, or even in a straight line with lengths of strong rope or chain hanging slack between them will also make suitable supports for clematis and roses, particularly some strong-growing types. *Clematis texensis* 'Duchess of Albany' should be given a rope to hang from in the author's opinion! She is extremely vigorous and demands space.

arches and pergolas by virtue of their siting in the garden (unless constructed close to a house or garden wall), do not provide shelter for plants. So these supports must be planted with hardy clematis. During my early days of gardening and growing clematis, I tended to choose vigorous varieties of clematis and other climbing plants in my enthusiasm for clothing such structures quickly. Experience has shown this to be a mistake, particularly in gardens with restricted space. A slow-growing variety may take longer to establish itself but will allow you greater scope for training the plant and growing different varieties on the same support. If choosing different varieties, take into consideration their pruning requirements. For example, it would be unwise to grow *Clematis viticella* 'Etoile Violette,' which requires hard pruning, with *Clematis macropetala*, which requires no pruning or very little tidying up or thinning out immediately after flowering. On the other hand, you may consider growing *C. viticella* 'Polish Spirit' with *C.* 'Comtesse de Bouchaud' or *C.* 'Huldine' as the pruning requirements are similar (Group 3, see page 36).

Propagation

Many a gem of clematis has found its way to global fame from the gardens of amateurs who grow clematis with great passion. It is quite easy to propagate some clematis and with a little care, attention, and an abundance of patience, excellent results are possible.

Propagation falls broadly into two major categories: sexual from seed, and asexual or vegetative from layers, cuttings, or division. New plants obtained by sexual method are all different, may resemble the parent but are not identical in all respects. On the other hand, plants raised by vegetative or asexual methods are carbon copies of their parents, barring sudden changes or mutations. Therefore, it is important to use vegetative methods to propagate selected fine forms of species and all named hybrids.

Seed

Seed can be either collected from your own plants or obtained from your friends or through the seed exchanges promoted by local and national clematis societies. If you are keen to collect seeds from your own plants, be sure they are ripe, usually brown in color, and dry. Readiness of the seeds for collection will depend on the time of flowering of clematis. Seeds of *C. montana, C. macropetala*, and *C. alpina* are normally ready for collection from late summer to early autumn, while many late-flowering species and hybrids will be ripened by mid to late autumn. If wet autumnal weather plays havoc with the seed heads, collect them and let them dry in a well-ventilated room, preferably unheated, before sowing or storing. Remember to append a label to the seed heads with the name of the species or hybrid and date of collection for your own reference.

Regardless of when, where, or from whom the ripened seed is obtained the best time to sow is immediately. However, if you cannot do so, store seeds carefully in an envelope until you are ready to sow. Remember to write down the name of the plant from which the seeds were collected and the date of collection.

Top left: Clematis seed may be fine and small (in the right hand) or large and easy to handle (in the left).

Top right and bottom: Once the seeds are placed on the surface of the compost, sieve some of the seed compost over to cover them lightly.

Materials required
Clematis seed, 3–4 in. (7.5–10 cm) pots, compost, coarse sand or grit, a small sieve, a large basin of water containing a small quantity of general purpose fungicide, a pane of glass, good quality labels, and a pencil.

Method
Fill the pot to within ½ in. (1 cm) of the top with pre-wetted and drained seed compost mixture. Firm gently with a flat piece of wood or the base of a smaller pot. Firming will ensure that there are no air spaces or hollows.

If the seeds carry feathery styles, cut them off without injuring the actual seed. Sow the seed evenly on the surface and avoid overcrowding. Allow at least ¼–½ in. (6–10 mm) spacing between seeds—the more the better.

Sieve just enough of the same seed compost on top to cover the seeds. Place a thin layer of coarse sand or grit on top of the sieved compost to prevent it drying out and minimize seed disturbance.

Stand the pot in a basin of water containing fungicide. Remove the pot from the water as soon as the sand or grit shows signs of dampness.

Label the pot clearly with the name of the seed and date of sowing. Place the pot either outside or in a cold greenhouse or coldframe, in a well-lit position but never in direct sunlight. It is important not to let the compost and seed dry out quickly.

Helpful Hints
If clay pots are used, be sure to cover the drainage holes with crocks or small stones before filling it with seed compost. Plastic pots do not require this treatment. Most hardy clematis germinate best in cool conditions.

Place a pane of glass over the pot to prevent disturbance by mice or birds if placed in the open garden. Note: It is important to check the pot at regular intervals to ensure the compost is moist but refrain from saturating it.

Germination of seed
When germination does take place it may very well be erratic over several months or, at the other extreme, it may be only a couple of weeks. If the seeds take a long time to germinate be patient; provided the seeds are viable and conditions such as air, moisture, and temperature are favorable for germination you will be rewarded.

Emergence of seedlings, growth, and potting-on

Keep an eye on the seedlings as they begin to emerge, but do not be in a hurry to transplant them. Let the seedlings produce two to three pairs of leaves and reach a height of about 2–3 in. (5–7.5 cm). Late summer is an ideal time to transplant because the seedlings tend to survive and thrive well. If the seedlings are not large enough to handle by the autumn, leave them well alone until the following spring. Remember to visit them and keep them moist, but slightly on the dry side during winter.

As soon as the seedlings are ready, they may be transplanted individually into 3 in. (7.5 cm) pots containing either loam-based or peat-based seedling compost. Before transplanting, water the pot of seedlings well; turn them all out together. Handle the seedlings with great care. Hold each seedling by the leaf and gently tease out the roots and transplant. Avoid touching the stem to prevent any damage or bruising to it. If germination is erratic and some seedlings are more advanced than others, you may wish to

transplant only the most advanced. Use a dibber to ease the roots out of the container, pull very gently by the leaves of the seedling with the aid of your thumb and finger. As soon as the seedlings are transplanted, label the pots individually with the name of the seedling and the date of transplanting.

Stand the pots either in a sheltered spot in the open garden or in a cold greenhouse, away from direct sunlight. As the transplanted seedlings settle down and grow away, pinch out the growing tips to encourage and assist the plants to become bushy. Insert a split cane, about 1½ ft (45 cm) long, into each pot at a short distance away from the main stem and tie in the new growths. Remember to water adequately and keep the compost moist at all times. Once the young clematis plants have established good root systems, the plants can be moved into bigger and deeper pots, approximately 9 in. (23 cm) in diameter, containing a suitable compost. Label the plants. Remember, aftercare of the plants is essential for successful results. Allow the plants to grow in their containers until they are well-established and ready to be given permanent places in the garden.

Good luck. Your efforts and patience may result in a plant or plants worthy of wider cultivation and pay off handsome dividends.

Maximizing the Plant.

The photographs opposite show how to bend a strong growing stem, one on either side of the main stem, run it along the ground, and tie the terminal shoot to a cane. The leaves at the nodal points (leaf joints) may be removed and the stems buried in the ground (see Layering). This manner of planting is ideal when a clematis is planted in association with a conifer.

Layering

Layering is a simple, natural form of vegetative propagation by which a shoot is induced to root while still remaining attached to the parent plant. Clematis with their pliable stems lend themselves admirably to this method of propagation. Even without any assistance from the gardener some self-layer, for example, *C.* x *jouniana* 'Praecox,' *C.* 'Fair Rosamond.' There are different methods of layering and the easiest one is simple layering.

Simple layering

Late spring to early summer, or late summer to early autumn are good times to attempt layering of clematis.

Layering directly into the ground

Dig a trench about 3 in. (7.5 cm) deep along one side of the plant where the stem will be placed. The length of the trench will depend on the number of plants you wish to propagate.

Place some organic compost or peat in the trench and mix it with the soil. Add a few handfuls of fine horticultural grit or coarse sand and gently mix it in.

Choose a vigorous, flexible stem, which can be bent down easily to soil level. Aim to bury two or three leaf joints (nodes) in the trench.

With the aid of a sharp knife, make a small oblique cut toward the base of the leaf joint and about ½ in. (1 cm) below it, slitting the node but taking care not to cut through it. If you are faint-hearted about this procedure leave the leaf joint intact. No harm will come and rooting will take place, albeit slowly. Remember plants do self-layer without slanting cuts!

If the slit has been made, dust the cut and the leaf joint with some hormone rooting powder. Prepare one or two further nodes in the same way. Peg the stem securely into the soil and cover the trench.

Insert a cane into the ground to accept the growing shoot tip and tie the top 1½ ft (45 cm) to the cane. Water the trench and the parent plant if necessary.

To prevent unwelcome visitors, such as cats and dogs, digging into the trench, make an elongated dome-shaped cover of chicken wire or stiff netting to protect the trench.

If there is not enough rainfall, water the trench and keep the stem beneath moist. The parent plant, too, should be watered during prolonged dry spells. The layer should be ready to be separated from the parent plant after twelve months or so.

Cut the part of the layered stem attached to the parent plant, free the new plantlet, dig it up carefully,

and place it in a pot containing compost, water it and let it grow. Remember to label and date your new plant.

Layering into a compost-filled pot

The main advantage of using a 4 in. (10 cm) pot for layering is that the new plant will root directly into it. There will be no damage to the root system when lifting the pot up from the soil. The plant can be moved to a bigger pot quite easily. The procedure is the same as the method for layering directly into the ground, except that the leaf joint is pegged directly into a compost-filled pot sunk into the ground. It is also important to check the pot regularly and ensure the compost is moist at all times. It is a good idea to use two or three pots and peg individual leaf joints into each pot to obtain two or three plantlets.

Cuttings

Amateur gardeners can propagate clematis, particularly the hybrids, from softwood or semi-ripe cuttings. Softwood of a plant is the youngest and greenest part of the growing stem, and the cuttings are usually taken in mid-spring to early summer and generally take about four to eight weeks to root. Semi-ripe cuttings are those taken from partially ripened wood, from mid-summer to early autumn. They take about eight to twelve weeks to root. The type of cutting normally employed to propagate clematis is known as an internodal cutting, that is, one in which the basal cut is made between two leaf joints (nodes).

Left:
Making a cutting from the midsection of a selected length of a clematis stem. The midsection is used because the tips will be too soft and the lower parts may be ripening or woody.

Above:
Make a clean cut just above the leaf joint or node and a second cut below the same joint.

Opposite:
After removing one of the pair of leaves from the leaf joint and half of the other to reduce moisture loss, the cuttings are immersed in a fungicide solution before being inserted into the compost filled pot. Note the leaf joints are at grit level.

Sharp penknife or blade, seed tray of small pots, fine horticultural grit or sand, cutting compost made up of equal parts of peat and grit or sand, general-purpose fungicide solution, fresh hormone rooting powder (optional), propagator or transparent plastic bags.

Method

Fill the pots with cutting compost, firm down and add a top layer of horticultural grit or sand. Water with a general-purpose fungicide and allow to drain.

Select two or three lengths of stems about 1–3 ft (30–90 cm) long on the parent plant and cut them above a leaf joint (node). Place them immediately in a transparent plastic bag. These will be the materials for your cuttings.

Take the cuttings from the midsections of the stems because the tips will be too soft and lower parts

may be ripening or woody. Cut through the stem immediately above a leaf joint and make a second cut about 1–2 in. (2.5–5 cm) below the same joint. Remove one of the pair of leaves from the leaf joint and half of the other to reduce moisture loss. The remaining leaves on the cutting should be clean and healthy to prevent any fungal infection. Immerse the cutting in a container of fungicide solution, allow to drain. If using hormone rooting powder, dip the bottom ½ in. (1 cm) of the cutting in it. Shake off any excess powder.

Insert each cutting into the compost until the leaf joint is at grit level and the lowest leaf is just above the surface.

Label the cuttings and include the date.

With the aid of a fine-grain sprinkler on a watering can, water the cuttings to eliminate any pockets of air and let the cuttings settle in comfortably. Make sure that you have added some general-purpose fungicide to the water.

The pot or pots of cuttings can now be placed in a propagator. If a propagator is not available, cover the individual pots with inverted polythene bags secured by elastic bands. The polythene cover will provide a humid environment. Bottom heat will accelerate the rooting process but is not essential. Keep the cuttings in a well-lit area but out of direct sunlight. Check on them regularly and remove any dead or infected material. Do not let the compost dry out.

Rooting should normally take about four weeks. Check whether the cutting has rooted by gently pulling on a leaf. If the cutting moves, then all is not well and you must give the cutting another week or two to establish more roots. Allow the cutting time to develop a strong root system before potting up. If the roots begin to grow out through the drainage holes at the bases of the pots, take the pots out of the propagator or remove the polythene bags. Let the cuttings, which are at this stage small plants, grow away in the pots for another couple of weeks and become strong.

Potting up

Pot each plant up in good quality loam-based compost in a 8 in. (20 cm or 2 liter) pot, burying the original leaf joint of the cutting slightly below the surface of the compost in the new pot. This is to encourage new shoots to break from the leaf joint. When the plant reaches a respectable height of 1 ft (30 cm), prune it back to just above the first pair of leaves immediately above the compost. This is to enable more sideshoots to break from the leaf joint. The plant can be allowed to grow and gain a height of about 1½ ft (45 cm) before being pruned back again to the second pair of leaves. While this repeated

**Opposite:
A pot of cuttings carefully placed in an inverted polythene bag to provide a humid environment to encourage rooting. Pots of cuttings can also be placed in a propagator if available. In that case a polythene bag would not be necessary.**

pruning may be discomforting to a novice propagator, it will result in a strong bushy plant. Water and feed the plant as and when necessary.

Planting out

It is advisable to grow the plant in its container and plant it out the following spring. If grown under glass, inside porches or even in well-lit rooms or on kitchen windowsills, harden it off gradually before planting it out.

Division

Herbaceous clematis, including *C. recta*, *C. integrifolia*, and *C. heracleifolia*, can be propagated by dividing the large clumps into smaller sections. Each section with a root system and one or more shoots or dormant buds will grow into a new plant. The method adopted is similar to the one used to divide herbaceous perennials in the garden.

The best time to divide the clumps is from late winter to early spring. Cut back any old top growths to the base and lift the plant out of the ground with a fork. If the clump is very large and heavy, get some help to lift it out. With the aid of a sharp spade or a strong carving knife, cut the clump into three or four sections. Replant each of these sections to grow into new plants.

A word of encouragement on propagation

Whatever method is used to propagate clematis, do not be disheartened if you fail the first time. Success will come your way as you become proficient in the techniques, especially those for propagation from cuttings. A few months ago, I took a softwood cutting of a very old *Clematis montana* growing in my neighbor's garden, simply inserted it directly into the soil in my garden and forgot all about it. The cutting rooted and I have a brand new plant. So propagating clematis—at least the less difficult ones—can be quite simple, not to mention fascinating and rewarding. Have a go, and above all, persevere!

Hybridization

Hybridization

Spotting a seedling of a garden plant that possesses some special characteristics or differs from its mother plant in some respects can be a thrilling experience for any gardener. If it turns out to be a winner so much the better. Nature is always busy and, as gardeners, there is no doubt we are grateful for all the surprises that come our way. Breeders of clematis are also constantly at work trying to come up with choice new varieties. This of course takes time, hard work, patience, an acute eye to spot something new or different and, more importantly, some background knowledge about the plants. However, for an amateur gardener dabbling in hybridizing it can be great fun.

A simple and easy approach to breeding a new clematis would be to gather and sow some seeds of your favorite clematis hybrids or cultivars and patiently wait for the seedlings to emerge, grow, and flower. The result will be potluck but, who knows, there may be just one seedling in many batches that turns out to be a winner. It is wise to remember that hybrids are really mongrels, so the accurate prediction of flower color and form is not that easy. Even when seeds of species clematis are sown, the progeny may be similar but not always identical to the mother plant. Variations are possible.

A planned breeding or hybridizing program may take a great deal of time and patience, but the final result may be very rewarding. The most vital first step is to list the aim of the exercise, for example , a compact, bushy, free-flowering clematis with small pendulous deep red flowers. Well-known and experienced clematis hybridizers, Vince and Sylvia Denny from Preston, England, listed the following special characteristics which must be taken into consideration before embarking on a deliberate clematis cross with a view to producing a good new hybrid: flower color, single or double blooms, height, disease resistance, bloom aspect, that is, whether the flower faces up, down or outward, root type—fibrous and fine or shoelace-like and thick—and, of course, beauty. Therefore, it pays to list the objectives and work toward achieving the best possible hybrid.

Hybridization

Top: The selected bud is opened very carefully by hand to expose the stamens and stigmas (male and female parts of the flower).

Center: Gently remove the tepals from the base of the bud. If faint hearted about removing the tepals choose a bud about to open and carefully snip away all the stamens before covering the emasculated flower with a muslin bag.

Bottom: All the stamens (anthers and filaments) are cut away with a pair of fine-pointed scissors. Take care not to cut into the base of the styles and stigmas (female organs).

Step-by-Step Guide to Successful Hybridization

Materials required

A pair of fine-pointed scissors, a small artist's camel's hair paint brush, muslin bags, fine twine or string, labels, a small notebook.

Parent selection

Choose two disease-free and strong-growing plants as "seed parent" (mother plant) and "pollen parent" (father plant). The stigma of the seed parent will receive the pollen grains from the anthers of the pollen parent.

Bud selection

Choose a plump bud on the seed parent, which is just about to open. A bud is normally chosen because pollinating agents, such as bees or butterflies, will not have had the opportunity to affect pollination.

Removal of tepals and stamens from the bud of the seed parent

Gently remove the unopened tepals from the base of the bud—not an easy exercise. Carefully

Above:
Raised and introduced by Bees of Chester in 1958, *Clematis* **'Bees Jubilee' is as popular as** *C.* **'Nelly Moser.' A prolific flowerer.**

Left: *Clematis* x *eriostemon* **'Hendersonii' is one of the earliest hybrids. A cross between** *C. integrifolia* **and** *C. viticella***, it is an outstanding variety with dark purple to dark blue flowers. An excellent plant for herbaceous or mixed borders.**

snip away all the stamens (filaments and anthers), using the scissors. Exercise caution to avoid cutting into the pistil (ovary, style, and stigma). Removal of stamens is essential to prevent self-pollination, that is, transfer of pollen grains from the anthers to the stigma of the same flower.

Covering the pistil of the seed parent

Gently insert the prepared emasculated flower bud into the muslin bag, close and tie the bag in place to prevent cross-pollination (transfer of pollen grains from another flower either on the same plant or from a different plant) by pollinating agents.

Preparation of the pollen parent

To ensure the pollen parent's stamens are completely free from pollen of other varieties accidentally brought in by visiting pollinating agents, select two flowers, remove the tepals carefully, insert each flower separately into a muslin or polythene bag, close and tie the bag. The second flower will act as a reserve just in case additional pollen is needed.

Left and below: When the stigma has ripened, pollen from the selected pollen parent is transferred to it with a camel's hair brush.

Opposite: The flower of the pollen parent is placed in a muslin bag to prevent visiting pollinating agents, like insects, depositing pollen from other varieties.

Examination of the stigma of the seed parent

After a few days, open the bag to see if the stigma is ready to receive the pollen. The stigma should appear shiny and covered with a viscous fluid. If it is ready, transference of the pollen grains from the pollen parent can commence. Otherwise, close and retie the bag and wait until the stigma becomes viscid and receptive.

Transfer of pollen to the stigma

Remove the bag from the prepared pollen parent and, with the aid of the camel's hair brush, lift and transfer the pollen from the anthers of the flower of the pollen parent to the stigma of the seed parent.

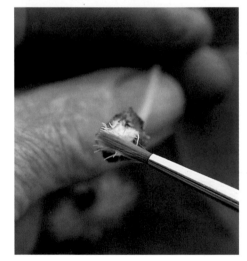

Covering the pollinated pistil of the seed parent

Rebag the pistil to prevent the stigma receiving unwanted and additional pollen from flowers of other clematis plants. To avoid condensation, leave a small air space when tying the bag.

Labeling and recording

Append a label securely to the seed parent with the names of the two parents and the date of pollination. Keep a record in the notebook for reference.

Repetition of the transference of pollen to the stigma

If in doubt about the success of the procedure to effect pollination, repeat it after two or three days by gathering the pollen with the brush from the reserve flower of the pollen parent. Be sure to cover the pollinated stigma of the seed parent. Even if there is no doubt that pollination has occured, repetition of the procedure is highly desirable.

Leave the bag covering the pollinated stigma of the seed parent in place for two or three weeks. If the pollination has been successful, fertilization (fusion of the male unit of the pollen with the female unit situated in the ovary) will have taken place. The ovaries will begin to swell gradually—a clear indication of the formation of seeds. Remove the bag to allow the sun and air to ripen the seeds. This may take three to four months. An additional secure label detailing information on the cross and the date on the stalk of the developing seed head is advisable.

A few weeks before collecting the seed head, cover it with a muslin bag even if the seeds are green, primarily to prevent accidental damage or loss, seed dispersal by wind, and also to protect the seed head from passing showers of rain. Wet or damp seed heads will not make for healthy storage later on.

Collecting, storing, and sowing the seeds

Keep an eye on the maturing seed head; the seeds will gradually change color from green to brown and the seed tails will develop. Note that viticella types do not develop fluffy seed tails. As the individual achenes begin to loosen, collect the seed head and place it in a paper bag or envelope and label it straight away. If the seed head was not covered and is damp, place it on a sheet of paper and leave it in a safe place so that it can dry. The seeds can be sown straight away or stored in a sealed polythene bag in a refrigerator for up to a year. Labeling the bag and recording the details of the contents in the notebook for future reference are essential. Take time to do both. For information on propagating clematis from seed see page 48.

Incidentally if the seed parent and pollen parent flower at different times—early and late, respectively, for example—and, if the aim is to make a cross between the two, then it is possible to gather the pollen from the pollen parent and store it in a clearly labeled airtight jar until the time is right for pollination of the seed parent's flower.

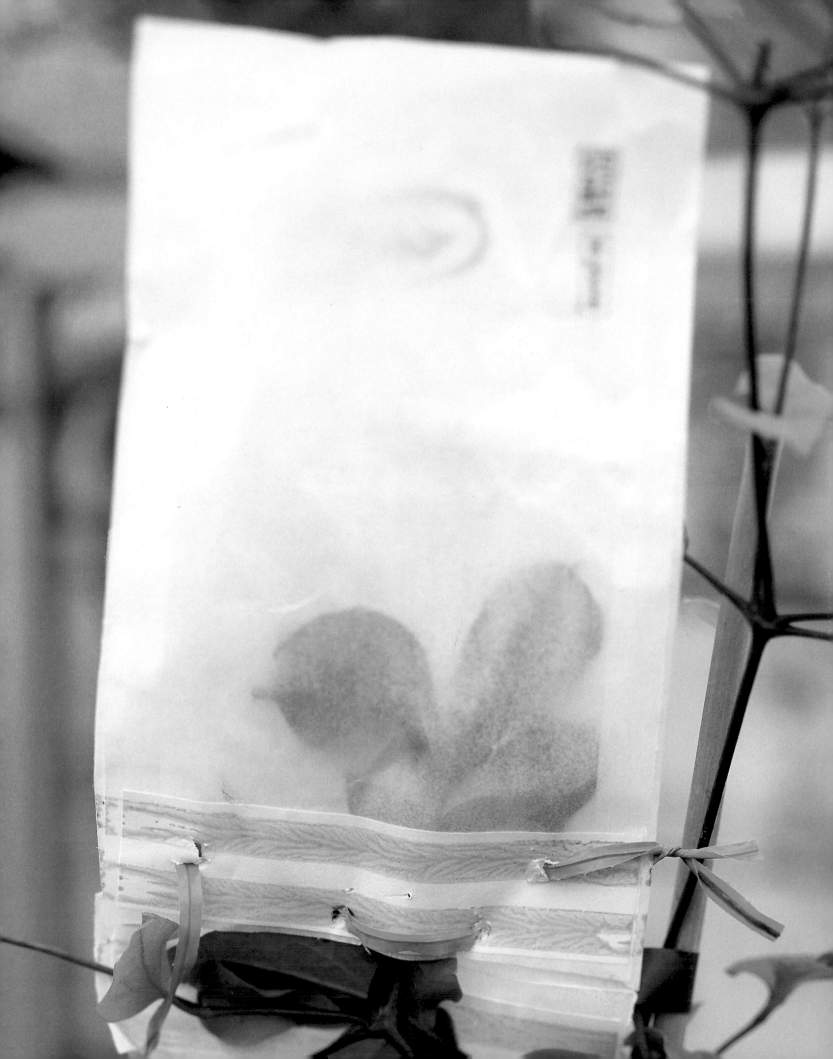

Naming and Registration Procedures for a New Hybrid

If the hybridization is successful and a worthwhile and exciting new hybrid is the result of all the patient and methodical work, the next step is to assess the plant. If you are in doubt, contact an experienced clematarian, specialist nursery grower, the International Clematis Society or British Clematis Society (see page 123), or a clematis society in your locality. All being well, proceed to name the plant in accordance with the International Code of Nomenclature for Cultivated Plants (1995) and also check with the Clematis Registrar of the International Clematis Registration Authority (see page 123) to ensure that the name chosen has not been given to another clematis. This is important because a name can only be used once and cannot be re-used even if the clematis is not in cultivation. As soon as the name has been approved by the Clematis Registrar the new hybrid can be recorded in the International Clematis Register. Introducing the new hybrid to the gardening public and propagating the plant for sale are the next steps. Good luck!

Secrets of Successful Hybridization

• Getting to know the plants, their distinguishing features and cultural requirements by building up a collection of clematis, species and hybrids, and growing them successfully for many years.
• Choosing your favorite hybrids and assessing what changes need to be made to produce even better ones.
• Recording the objective clearly.
• Making a series of crosses between the plants selected for hybridization.
• Keeping complete and accurate notes about the number of crosses, parentage, dates, results, and any comments.
• Having time and patience.
• Selecting the very best hybrid and discarding the useless ones without shedding tears.

Interspecific Hybrids?

While it is encouraging that so much effort and time are being given to introduction of new hybrids by crossing hybrids with hybrids, there are also opportunities for interspecific hybrids, that is, making crosses between dif-

Opposite: *Clematis cirrhosa* 'Lansdowne Gem' is a sport of *C. cirrhosa* 'Freckles.' It was discovered and named by M. L. Jerard of New Zealand in 1995 and introduced in 1997. An evergreen variety.

Above: *Clematis macropetala* 'Albina Plena' is an early flowering variety worth growing in association with other garden shrubs. No excessive pruning or there will be a loss of flowers.

ferent but compatible species. Recently this area has been considerably neglected. A knowledge of the chromosonal numbers (see Glossary, page 122) of different species of clematis will enable you to choose the correct plants to make the crosses. Even if that information is not available, trial and error can lead to exciting new hybrids.

A Word of Caution on New Hybrids

At the moment there are well over 1,000 named hybrids of clematis and more and more are being added to the list each year, which begs the question about their merit as garden plants. Some of the "new" named varieties are barely distinguishable from existing ones. Call it "just another blue or purple." How many of these look-alike varieties does a gardener really need? How many have really undergone proper "trials"

before being named and introduced as a worthwhile hybrid? In the author's opinion far too many chance seedlings and sports of clematis are being offered for sale without being tried and tested. Dedicated and experienced breeders of clematis usually take up to ten years to select and introduce a new cultivar. Quite a number of amateur hybridists have given us some wonderful plants in the past. So by all means have a go at hybridization but set out to produce really good varieties with some "extra" distinguishing feature or features and not just another blue or purple or a double!

If you believe you have a worthwhile hybrid, then send it to the British Clematis Society's International Trial Ground (see page 122) for trial. This will ensure that only the very best hybrid will find its way to the gardener.

Pests, Diseases, and Disorders

"One snail too many," "a healthy clematis just collapsed," "the leaves look yellow," "the buds are all eaten by some culprit." How often I hear these statements from gardeners who grow clematis with love and attention. The aim should be to prevent as many problems as possible by adopting good basic principles of cultivation and care.

Pests

Aphids (greenfly, blackfly)
These may be winged or wingless insects, multiply very quickly and are usually found in clusters on stems, buds, and the undersides of leaves. Leaves become stunted and distorted. Since they cause damage by sucking the sap from young shoots, leaves, and buds, it is important to deal with them quickly. Use a systemic insectide before heavy infestations develop. Excessive dryness at the roots is conducive to aphid infestation. It is important to keep container-grown and garden plants moist at all times. Water around the base of the plants thoroughly. Note that pesticide resistance in some aphids is widespread.

Whiteflies
Usually plants grown in greenhouses or conservatories are affected by whiteflies—small, winged white insects, which rest on the undersides of leaves and fly off when the plants are disturbed. Counter the pest by biological control with the parasitic wasp, *Encarsia formosa* if possible; otherwise, spray with a suitable pesticide. However, there are pesticide-resistant strains of greenhouse white fly, and it is a difficult pest to eradicate.

Aphids, commonly known as greenflies or blackflies, usually attack young buds, leaves, and shoots. Deal with these pests quickly.

Winter moth caterpillars
The light green caterpillars of the winter moth (*Operophtera brumata*) are active during late winter and early spring. They feed voraciously on the leaves between bud burst and late spring. Early flower buds in the axils may also be severely damaged. Remove the caterpillars before they devour the leaves and buds. Spray with an appropriate pesticide (Derris) as soon as possible after bud burst.

Ghost swift moth caterpillars
The caterpillars of the ghost swift moth (*Hepialus humuli*) may be an occasional problem in some gardens. The wings of the male moth are snow-white above, and brownish black beneath, while those of the female are dull yellow with a brick-red border and central spots. The wingspan is about 2 in. (5 cm). The caterpillar is creamish yellow with a reddish brown head, the coloring spreading to the region immediately behind the head. It feeds upon the roots of clematis and some other garden plants, although it feeds predominantly on nettles. Most damage is done between late summer and mid-spring and the plants show signs of poor growth or wilt during spring.

Keeping the garden or adjacent areas nettle-free will help to control the caterpillar damage. It may be necessary to uproot plants that show signs of poor growth or wilt to see if the caterpillars are present. If so, they should be collected and destroyed. If the damage is not too severe, it is advisable to replant the clematis in another part of the garden.

Vine weevils (*Otiorhynchus sulcatus*)
These widespread and destructive general garden pests can be a problem during clematis propagation and for plants in containers. Vine weevils are really beetles, characterized chiefly by the possession of a rostrum, a distinct beak-like prolongation of the head. Adult weevils are grayish black, not very shiny, measuring just under ½ in. (1 cm) in length. They are flightless, feed on leaves by night, and hide during the daytime. Their mouthparts are well-adapted for chewing; hence the irregular "U" shaped notches in the margins of leaves and flowers. Unlike caterpillars and slugs, vine weevils are incapable of making holes in the leaf blades. One weevil is enough to start a major infestation, and it is the larval stage in its life cycle that is most damaging to the roots of plants. The larvae (grubs), about ⅜ in. (9 mm) long, are plump and creamy white with brown heads and no legs. They are easily identified by their characteristic "C" shape.

The larvae usually emerge after two weeks from tiny eggs laid by the adults from early summer onward and commence feeding voraciously on the roots of the host plants. Most of the damage to the plants is caused during autumn, winter, and early spring. Young clematis plants under attack by vine weevil larvae usually do not recover because the roots are damaged or well and truly eaten. However, mature plants with a well-established root system may withstand a certain amount of damage and recover, provided adequate and effective control measures are put in place.

Once the notches in the leaves are identified, they are the indicators of adult weevils at work. Spraying the foliage of plants with a proprietary insecticide may help to kill the weevils, the aim being to prevent the adults from laying their eggs below the surface of the soil, or compost in the case of container-grown plants. Thankfully, composts treated with suitable chemicals to deal with the larvae are now available and should be used, where possible, for container planting.

Otherwise, control by biological methods is the only option. These include the use of parasitic nematodes (eelworms), which work their way into the bodies of the vine weevil larvae and kill them by releasing bacterial toxin. For the nematodes to be effective, the soil temperatures should be between 50°F (10°C) and 59°F (14°C). Therefore, treatment of plants with nematodes is more effective in heated greenhouses and conservatories than in the garden. Outdoor applications can be made during late summer and early autumn when the soil temperatures do not fall below 59°F (14°C).

Precautionary measures, such as examining the rootballs of newly purchased container-grown plants before planting, are advisable. Always buy strong healthy plants. Nightly visits to the garden, conservatory, and greenhouse to collect the weevils by hand means fewer eggs laid and less larval damage to the roots.

The wilting and eventual collapse of plants resulting from excessive damage to the roots should not be confused with the problem of clematis wilt.

Earwigs hide by day but feed actively on buds and flowers by night. Keep a watchful eye on them and collect as many as you can.

Earwigs

Yellowish brown insects, easily identified by a pair of curved pincers at the posterior end. They hide by day and feed actively at night on leaves and tepals of flowers. They also damage flowerbuds by boring holes into them. Damage can be limited by placing inverted pots that have been loosely stuffed with moss, straw, or hay on canes among plants. The earwigs use these as their hiding places during the daytime. Collect, remove and destroy these insects by dropping them into salty water.

Red spider mites

There are many different species of these eight-legged pests but the most common one is the two-spotted or greenhouse red spider mite (*Tetranychus urticae*). They are not a major problem in the garden but they thrive in dry conditions in greenhouses and conservatories. The infested leaves become dull, yellow, speckled on the upper surface, and eventually fall. Close examination may reveal a fine silky cobweb covering the leaves of plants heavily infested with red spider mites. Maintenance of high humid conditions in the greenhouse and conservatory will help to prevent red spider mite attack on some tender clematis plants. Spray the undersides of leaves with water regularly.

Leaf-mining insect

It is the larval stage of the agromyzid fly (*Phytomyza vitalaba*) that occurs on the native clematis, *Clematis vitalba*. It is unlikely to be a damaging pest unless the level of infestation is very heavy. The fly larva makes a sinuous tunnel through the upper surface of the leaf, which means the mine is scarcely visible on the underside of the leaf. The mines usually terminate in a small irregular blotch. Excrement can be seen within the mine and is deposited as a near continuous line along one edge of the mine. The color of the mines can be white or brown, and they are largely situated close to the leaf margins. Leaves of *texensis* hybrids and, occasionally, *macropetalas* and *alpinas* are affected. If the activity of the leaf-mining insect causes concern, it could be controlled by either removing mined leaves or by spraying with an appropriate pesticide when signs of the infestation are first seen.

Snails and slugs

Small, big, fat, long , short, black, pinkish white, slimy—these shelled or naked nocturnal creatures devour young shoots, stems, leaves, buds, and flowers of clematis. They eat their way through soft, juicy, tender parts of the plant, and even succeed in stripping the outer layers of young and old stems of clematis. The rasping tongues of snails and slugs must never be underestimated. They set out to work at night soon after showers of rain, and humid conditions encourage them to feed voraciously. They may not be as agile as vine weevils but are nifty climbers, almost competing with the climbing habits of clematis. This means no part of clematis is safe from their jaws.

From the author's experience, placing a thick layer of horticultural grit mixed with sand around the bases of plants will help to minimize the damage. Inverted empty halves of grapefruits placed here and there among plants in the garden will attract them. Once they congregate inside the grapefruit halves they can be collected and dealt with.

Shoots of newly planted and young clematis which emerge from below soil level during early spring can be protected with shields made from large, transparent plastic soft-drink bottles from which the top ends have been cut away. The protective covers should be removed as the shoots make their way upward but take other precautions to prevent the snails and slugs from attacking them.

Nightly visits to the garden to remove them, bag them, and perhaps let them free elsewhere may also be a solution. Encourage a couple of friendly hedgehogs to take up residence in the garden. Frogs are also quite partial to slugs.

If none of the above appeals, then you can resort to scattering metaldehyde slug pellets. Watering the leaves with sluggit solution may also help. As a result of snail and slug activity, stems or parts of stems of clematis may be severed. This will cut off water and other nutrients to the stems, resulting in withering and collapse. Do not confuse with clematis wilt.

Goats, rabbits, cats, mice, and moles

"My neighbor's goats in the field next-door actually put their front feet on the trellis which supports *Clematis* 'Bill Mackenzie' and stripped poor 'Bill' of all his top growth," a lady gardener wrote to me. So beware!

If you garden in areas with a rabbit population, take care to prevent them eating all the top growths of your clematis. Cylind-rical cages made out of fine-mesh chicken wire or lengths of drain pipes may be used to protect the clematis shoots from rabbit attacks. Take care to bury these barriers well below the soil level so that the rabbits do not burrow their way under them to consume the new shoots.

Cats are not really pests but they have a habit of breaking some new shoots of clematis—their playful activity leading to a sort of pruning. If there are cats, mice won't be a problem. If there are no cats to deal with the mice, they will gnaw the stems, especially during winter months, and transport pieces of them for nesting purposes. Such gnawing may result in the permanent severence of the stems from the crown of roots. Deep planting of large-flowered hybrids will ensure new shoots being thrown up from below soil level. If the garden is not very big, judicious setting of mouse traps will help to catch the culprits. In very large country gardens, opt for strong and vigorous species and hybrids of clematis. As the girth of the stems increases with age mice will not be able to chew through them.

Moles are little horrors in country gardens. They are capable of destroying the whole root system of clematis. Mole scarers may help. If moles are a major problem, recruit the services of professional "mole trappers."

Diseases

Organisms, such as bacteria, fungi, or viruses, may be the cause of some diseases in clematis although bacterial diseases are rare.

Slime flux

This condition is comparatively rare in clematis. *Clematis montana* and, occasionally, *viticella* hybrids are affected. A foul-smelling, white to pinkish, creamy or slimy and frothy exudation near the base of the stems oozes down and collects in a puddle on the soil surface around the plant. The vile smell and discoloration are due to the fermentation of the exuding sugary sap from the cracked or injured stems by large numbers of bacteria.

The cause is thought to be due to injury to the stem (stem cracks), often through spring frost when sap pressure is high and just before the foliage buds burst. Hard-pruned stems of some clematis tend to suffer from slime flux immediately after severe frost as well.

Clematis wilt and leaf spot

Clematis wilt is a well-known and much discussed fungal disease, which affects only the large-flowered hybrids. The causal pathogen is *Phoma clematidina*. The fungi enter the clematis stem through the leaf joints (nodes), invariably at or just above soil level. However, the pathogenic fungi can gain entry through a leaf joint at a higher level on the main stem or a side branch of a stem. They may even be present on the leaves of clematis, causing leaf-spots, which are frequently brown in color.

The worrying damage occurs when the fungi attack a stem or stems. The result is the notorious and heart-breaking sudden wilting and collapse of a hitherto healthy stem or stems or, at times, even the whole plant. In my experience, sudden rises in temperature and humidity seem to play an important part in the onset of clematis wilt. Once the fungi have gained entry they destroy the living nodal tissue, thereby stopping the transport of water and nutrients to the rest of the stem above the point of

---

As soon as this condition is spotted, remove the affected stems, cutting well back into healthy stems, to ground level if necessary. Mulch, feed, and water the plants well. Unless the slime flux is very severe, it is seldom that the whole plant succumbs to death. Do not uproot the plants in a hurry. New shoots may emerge from below soil level. Mulching the plants to conserve moisture is advisable.

Mildew

Mildew is a fungal disease that affects a variety of plants and in clematis some varieties are more prone to it than others, including texensis hybrids, C. 'Star of India,'

C. 'Durandii,' C. 'Perle d'Azur.' The disease spreads rapidly in mild weather and in conditions of shade and poor air circulation. Mildew can also be a major problem in over-planted sheltered gardens.

The fungal growth, usually white and powdery, appears on leaves and stems. Leaves become yellow and fall early, the plants look unsightly and in severe cases of infection even buds and flowers become distorted. It is important to avoid dry and excessively shady sites for planting. Mulching and regular watering, par-

Above: Slime flux. The oozing of the white to pinkish, creamy and frothy substance from the stems of the *montana* collects in a puddle on the soil surface giving off a foul smell.

ticularly around the base of the plant, are necessary to avoid mildew. Unfortunately, infected plants are a source of infection. Where possible, try to avoid planting too close to walls and remember, the greater the air circulation, the less the infection.

If the problem is persistent you may have to resort to chemical control. Spray early in the season and at regular intervals with suitable and, preferably, systemic fungicide.

infection. As a result, that part of the stem carrying leaves, buds, and flowers withers, turns black, then brown and dies. The portion of the stem below the infected node however, remains green and healthy. The fungi can attack plants any time from late spring to mid-summer.

Disappointment at such an attack should not delay the cutting back of any affected stem or stems to healthy green tissue and incineration of the wilted parts. As a precaution against further attacks, drench the area around the base of the plant with a fungicide such as carbendazim after watering the plant well. Repeat at regular intervals as new shoots and leaves begin to grow. Pinching out the growth tips will encourage the stems to generate sideshoots. The aim should be to establish a healthy woody framework and make the plants wilt-resistant.

Although some large-flowered hybrids are martyrs to wilt, in my experience they learn to grow out of the nasty habit of wilting and grow into strong, healthy plants and flower well. *Clematis* 'Niobe' is a prime example. There is a school of thought that large-flowered varieties with *C. lanuginosa* in their pedigree tend to be high wilters.

Should any of your large-flowered clematis persist in frustrating you by succumbing to wilt year after year, get rid of them and invest in a good small-flowered *viticella* hybrid. Ideally, avoid planting your new clematis in the site occupied by the wilter because fungal spores may be present. However, if you must use the same area, remove as much soil as possible from the site, replace it with good quality topsoil or compost, and proceed with the planting. If the clematis is a large-flowered hybrid remember to deep-plant it—the surface of the rootball should be at least 2½ in. (6 cm) below soil level. As a precautionary measure, drench the planted site with more of the fungicide solution. Do not use the same fungicide over a long period of time because the fungus can develop immunity to it.

Strange as it may sound, some clematis varieties simply refuse to settle down in certain gardens, wilting annually. Yet the same varieties may present no problems in another garden. Two or three stems of *Clematis* 'H.F. Young' with plump buds about to burst open into handsome blue flowers insist on wilting each year in my garden and yet present no problem in the garden of a friend. The vagaries of performance may be inexplicable but no gardener should be deterred from planting and enjoying as many varieties of clematis as possible because of clematis wilt.

When it strikes a large flowered cultivar, clematis wilt has no mercy. Remove all wilted stems, buds, and flowers immediately and burn them. Soaking the soil around the clematis with a general purpose fungicide may be helpful although there is not as yet a permanent cure for genuine clematis wilt.

Disorders

Nutritional and mineral deficiencies, unsatisfactory or unsuitable growing conditions, including atmospheric factors, may lead to physiological disorders in clematis.

Drought and irregular water supply

Most clematis are moisture-loving plants. Premature autumn coloring, loss of leaves, stunted growth, poor, misshapen and undersized flowers, temporary and permanent wilting, and even die-back may be the direct result of drought and irregular water supply. It is essential to use moisture-retentive mulch and water the plants regularly. Pay special attention to the water requirements of plants growing in light, sandy soils, of young, newly planted clematis and of those growing in containers. However, all clematis plants, irrespective of their age and with the exception of a few Mediterranean and New Zealand species and hybrids that prefer moderately dry conditions, require adequate amounts of water to grow and flower satisfactorily. Do not assume that plants will only need water during very hot summer months. Spring can be dry and it is important to water the plants as the sap rises and fresh new growths begin to appear.

Magnesium deficiency

Clematis fed heavily on high-potash fertilizers, such as tomato feed, to promote flowering, tend to suffer from magnesium deficiency. Heavy rainfalls and excessive watering also leach out magnesium from the soil, thus making it unavailable to the plants. Plants grown in extremely acidic soil also suffer from magnesium deficiency. The symptoms are readily noticed in the leaves, which become yellow, particularly between the veins, resulting in premature leaf fall.

Treat plants and soil with Epsom salts (magnesium sulphate) during autumn. Add the salts directly to the soil at the rate of 1 oz per 10 sq ft (25 g per sq m), or dissolve 7½ oz salts in 2¼ gallons of water (210 g salts in 10 liters) and apply as a foliar spray. Add a wetting agent, such as dish-washing liquid, when making up the solution.

Bright sunlight

Some flowers of clematis, notably the pink ones, including C. 'Nelly Moser,' bleach and fade in very bright sunlight. Avoid planting such varieties in south or west-facing aspects.

An early flowering variety, *Clematis* 'Miss Bateman' is a prolific flowerer and an easy variety to grow.

Reduced daylight hours and low temperatures

Some early-flowering clematis may not color up fully and as a result the tepals appear green. There is nothing wrong with the plants or flowers. As enough light becomes available and the temperature rises the tepals will color up and the flowers will look beautiful.

Premature brown leaves

In some clematis, for example, C. 'Hagley Hybrid,' the lower older leaves turn brown early on in their life and remain on the stems, no doubt presenting an undesirable sight. There seems to be no definite explanation for this unfortunate leaf habit, although various theories, including old age of the leaves, have been put forward. Growing such clematis up and through evergreen shrubs will hide those unsightly brown leaves from the gardener's eyes. Drought or water shortage may also cause the leaves to brown, wither, and fall prematurely.

Helpful Hints

Suitable systemic insecticide and fungicide containing primicarb and buprimate with triforine is available to gardeners. It controls aphids, including greenfly, blackfly, and mildew. It also protects plants from aphid and disease attack. Exercise maximum care when dealing with pesticides.

Courageous Clematis

In conclusion, despite the list of pests, diseases, and disorders listed above, in my experience, clematis are relatively trouble-free plants. I am constantly amazed to see plants I had inadvertently neglected fight back and surprise me by flaunting their buds and flowers. Excessive kindness is as bad as neglect: over-feeding and over-watering (water adequately is the message) may result in unnecessary loss of plants. *Clematis* x *aromatica*, for example, does not like too much water. The roots tend to rot. Never be afraid to transplant (see page 27), preferably when the plants are dormant, if you have chosen the wrong site. With a bit of care and luck you will succeed. I have managed to transplant five or six-year-old plants without great difficulty. Good gardeners usually learn through trial and error that plants have a considerable capacity to adjust, settle down, and cooperate to deliver their best. I firmly believe in talking to my clematis and other plants in my garden. They seem to listen and reward me.

Plant Directory

Of the 200 and more species and about a thousand named hybrids of clematis, it is only possible to include a small number of what is generally available to the gardener in the following pages. In the recent past, many new hybrids have been named. Furthermore, with the popularity of clematis as a garden plant climbing new heights, the hybridizers are busy introducing new varieties each year.

There are a number of clematis specialist nurseries in the United Kingdom and many offer mail-order service. Varieties from Holland, Sweden, Latvia, Estonia, Poland, Russia, Japan, and New Zealand are also becoming widely available to gardeners. I have endeavored to cover some of the best clematis—both species and hybrids—suitable for growing in different climes of the clematis-growing world.

I have also taken into consideration the hardiness, flowering times, pruning requirements, and propagation of clematis in assembling the directory of clematis, the aim being to assist the gardener in growing as many different varieties of clematis as possible with ease and confidence. In the entries about individual plants, I have included only information that is most pertinent. For example, I have mentioned propagation either to point out the most successful method or to alert the gardener to the fact that a particular clematis may present a challenge. In the cases of clematis where propagation is not referred to, any of the methods described on pages 47-54 will produce good results. If features, such as flower size, anthers or seedheads, are eye-catching or remarkable, I have pointed them out.

In gardens which enjoy a mild and maritime climate, flowering may start as early as mid-winter and continue well into late autumn. Even then, the vagaries of weather may play havoc with the early spring-flowering varieties. Depending on the weather, the pattern of flowering may even vary from year to year. The amount of sunshine during spring and summer may also dictate the flower color, and all too often the tepals may fail to color properly, or may even remain green. The height of the plants may also vary from garden to garden and locality to locality. In countries that have long, severely cold winters, the flowering season may be shorter, but there are a number of hardy clematis that will give a good display during the growing season. Therefore, choosing the right species or hybrid to suit the growing conditions and location is very important.

Clematis can also be grown as conservatory, greenhouse, and alpine house plants, almost throughout the year. The New Zealand species and their many hybrids are ideally suited for growing under glass in cool-temperate regions, although some may also be grown in open gardens in places where frost is not a major problem.

Gardeners often ask me to recommend evergreen clematis and therefore I have dealt with this group of plants first in the directory. The contents of the Plant Directory do not follow the strict botanical classification of clematis. I make no apologies for adopting a format more suited to gardeners' needs.

Note: Clematis marked (PBR) are protected by Plant Breeder Rights in the EU. Unlicenced Propagation Prohibited.

Plant Hardiness Zones

Hardiness is often difficult to quantify, for the simple reason that it depends on the severity of the cold weather and its timing. Unexpected and most unusual freezing weather conditions in early winter a few years ago destroyed *Clematis forsteri* in my normally frost-free maritime garden. However, all plants in the Plant Directory carry a zonal range—the lower number indicating the lowest winter temperatures the plants will be able to withstand and survive, while the higher one relates to the hottest in which plants will grow well and give a good account of themselves. Most clematis are hardy plants which means they should be able to withstand temperatures down to 5°F (-15°C).

Range of average annual minimum temperature for each climatic zone developed by the United States Department of Agriculture (USDA)

	Temperature Range	
Zone	°F	°C
1	below -50	below -45.5
2	-50 to -40	-45.5 to -40.1
3	-40 to -30	-40.0 to -34.5
4	-30 to -20	-34.4 to -28.8
5	-20 to -10	-28.8 to -23.4
6	-10 to 0	-23.3 to -17.8
7	0 to +10	-17.7 to -12.3
8	+10 to + 20	-12.2 to -6.7
9	+20 to + 30	-6.6 to -1.2
10	+30 to + 40	-1.1 to + 4.4
11	Above + 40	Above + 4.4

Evergreen Species and Hybrids
(Pruning Group 1)

All early to late spring-flowering evergreen and deciduous clematis flower on old wood or growths made during the previous year. Prune them only when necessary, and immediately after flowering, by removing excessive side growths and without cutting back the framework of old wood. However, if the plants have been allowed to grow vigorously and without any light pruning or tidying up over a number of years and reach the stage when they need to be disciplined and controlled, it would be advisable to prune back to a main framework of old wood as soon as the flowering period is over and preferably during late spring. This drastic action encourages new shoots to break from the old wood, grow and get sufficiently ripened during the warm summer months to produce flowers the following year. If the cutting back takes place later in the year, there will be a loss of flowers during the following spring.

Clematis armandii **'Apple Blossom'** is a scented evergreen variety; it needs space to grow well and flower. Not for exposed cold gardens.

Clematis armandii
1900

Introduced to England from China by Ernest Wilson. This is a vigorous handsome plant requiring considerable growing space. The juvenile leaves are pinkish bronze, becoming dark green, glossy, and somewhat leathery in texture as they mature. They are usually trifoliate with the middle leaflet being larger. *C. armandii* is best planted in a sunny and sheltered position in the garden, preferably against a wall or strong fence to minimize frost and wind damage to the leaves and maximize flowering capacity. Clusters of white or creamy white scented flowers are borne in great profusion on ripened old wood of the previous year's growth. Since the plant is evergreen and flowers on old wood, it is important not to prune away the old wood. However, careful removal of some of the excessively long side growths immediately after flowering will keep the plant under control, as well as enabling the new stems to ripen and be ready to flower the following spring. It is fairly hardy and will withstand temperatures as low as 14°F (-10°C). Cut flowers of *armandii* in a vase indoors will fill the room with its beautiful scent.

Flowering season: mid to late spring.

Height and spread: up to 33 ft (10 m). Propagation from cuttings difficult, from seed variable; layering recommended.

Zones: 6–9.

Clematis armandii 'Apple Blossom'
Growth habit similar to that of *C. armandii*. Pink buds opening to whitish pink scented flowers.

Clematis armandii 'Bowl of Beauty'
White, bowl-shaped and scented flowers.

Clematis armandii 'Jefferies'
Long, pointed leaves and white, scented flowers; there is a summer flowering occasionally, in addition to the normal spring display.

Clematis armandii 'Snowdrift'
According to Raymond Evison, the true form of this hybrid should have blunt rounded leaflets and white, fully rounded flowers.

Clematis australis

A New Zealand species. The leaves are dark green and trifoliate. The creamy white or yellow star-shaped flowers, single or in clusters, are slightly nodding and scented. This clematis is not very hardy but makes a good conservatory plant.

Flowering season: mid to late spring.
Height: up to 6½ ft (2 m).
Propagate: from cuttings.
Zone: 8.

Clematis x cartmanii 'Joe'
Circa 1980

Named after Joe Cartman of New Zealand. This is a cross between *C. marmoraria* and *C. paniculata*. Foliage is dense, dark green, and finely divided. The prolific flowers smother and hide almost all of the foliage. They are partially nodding and white with creamy yellow stamens. In all but extremely cold and frosty gardens, 'Joe' can be grown horizontally as a rockery plant by pegging down the stems or can be allowed to cascade or form a mound.

It is hardy to 23°F (-5°C). If grown as a container plant in a greenhouse and given a cane as support it can reach up to 6½ ft (2 m) but must be trained and tied to the cane. Well-trained plants of 'Joe' in full flower are often exhibited in the alpine section of horticultural shows.

Flowering season: mid to late spring.
Height: up to 6½ ft (2 m) if grown with support.
Propagate: from cuttings.
Zones: 7–9.

Clematis cirrhosa
1590s

A Mediterranean plant introduced into England in 1590. It is a very variable species. Ideally, it should be planted and grown in a sheltered, sunny site to encourage flowering from the previous season's ripened stems. The leaves are dark green and glossy. Nodding flowers are somewhat bell-shaped and creamy white with greenish stamens. Reddish brown blotches or spots may be present in the tepals. *C. cirrhosa* should be grown in dry soils in a well-drained site. Heidi Gildemeister, a pio-

neer of waterwise gardening, says that the plant is drought-tolerant and need not be watered during dry summers. In the wild the plant goes into a period of rest during the summer. In the author's garden, where the plant grows against a sunny south-facing wall, there is no active summer growth. It is not very hardy. A severe winter will kill the plant, except when grown in mild areas.

Flowering season: late autumn to mid-spring.
Height: up to 14¾ ft (4.5 m).
Propagate: propagation is not difficult as plants come up readily from fresh seed.
Zones: 7–9.

Clematis cirrhosa var. balearica

Leaves: finely divided and bronze-green during winter. Flowers: pale cream with reddish maroon blotches within.

Clematis cirrhosa 'Wisley Cream'

Resembles the species cirrhosa. It is shy to flower. There are no blotches on the flowers.

Clematis cirrhosa 'Freckles'

A very good plant with large cream flowers with intensely reddish maroon to violet-purple spots or blotches. It tends to go into summer dormancy. The main crop of flowers is from late autumn to early winter, although in the author's garden it flowers well into mid or late winter.

Note on *Clematis cirrhosa*
A high pergola or an arch in a sunny part of the garden would be ideal for growing all the *cirrhosas* in localities which are not subjected to severe frost. This will enable the gardener to enjoy the nodding flowers by looking up into them. When grown against a wall, the markings or blotches on the inside of the flowers are not fully visible to the gardener's eyes. The only disadvantages of clothing an arch or a pergola with an evergreen clematis is that rain drips will fall on you should you wish to walk beneath the structure after a rainfall, and the plant will need routine maintenance.

Clematis alpina 'Willy' flowers during spring and is one of the first *alpinas* to come into flower.

Clematis alpina 'Ruby' may be vigorous but site this variety carefully so that the flowers will look vibrant in the sunshine.

Alpina and Macropetala Species and Hybrids
(Pruning Group 1)

Both species and hybrids of alpinas and macropetalas are very hardy and well-suited for growing in exposed and sheltered gardens. They can be grown on their own and trained on suitable supports or through strong shrubs and small trees. It is not always necessary to grow these plants vertically: if a suitable pocket of soil is available for planting in gardens where there are natural outcrops of rocks, these plants will look most effective cascading down; compact varieties look good when grown in large containers.

The flowers of alpinas have a central large boss of white staminodes, the outer ones being longer and spoon-shaped, surrounded by four tepals, while those of macropetalas have numerous, almost layers of, staminodes, which confer a semi-double to double appearance on the flowers. Growth habits of both species are similar. Roots are very fine (fibrous). Handle the rootball carefully and do not disturb the roots when planting. Once planted they establish very quickly and do not suffer from clematis wilt. The main crop of flowers appears between mid and late spring and the plants flower intermittently during summer and early autumn. Seed heads are most attractive when shimmering in the sunshine. They are easily propagated from cuttings, seed, and layering.

Alpinas (Pruning Group 1)

Clematis alpina 'Columbine'

Flowers: almost bell-like, pale lavender blue with long and pointed tepals.
Staminodes: white.
Flowering season: mid to late spring.
Height: about 8 ft (2.5 m).
Zones: 3–9.

Clematis alpina 'Frances Rivis'

This is a very popular clematis. Flowers: deep blue (do not be put off by the pinky color on the labels attached to the plant for sale) with long, slightly twisted, tepals.
Flowering season: mid to late spring.
Height: 6½–10 ft (2–3 m).
Zones: 3–9.

Clematis alpina 'Frances Rivis' has a glorious abundance of cascading blue flowers.

Clematis alpina 'Ruby'

Soft reddish pink flowers, vibrant when grown in full sun. This is a very vigorous plant; if growing through another shrub or tree, choose a strong-growing plant in the garden. It is advisable to remove a few side growths each year immediately after flowering, once the framework is established.

Flowering season: mid to late spring.
Height: 10–13 ft (3–4 m).
Zones: 3–9.

Other recommended alpinas

'Helsingborg' for blue-purple blooms; 'Tage Lundell' for rose-purple; 'Jacqueline du Pre' for rosy-mauve pink; and 'White Moth' for white.

Clematis alpina 'Helsingborg' is a Swedish cultivar which is well worth growing for its abundance of beautfully shaped flowers.

Macropetalas (Pruning Group 1)

Clematis macropetala

It is well worth finding room for this plant in the garden. Flowers are borne singly and are nodding and pale blue with a shade of violet red. The beauty of these flowers is enhanced by the petal-like staminodes. These are numerous and in many rows, with the outer long ones taking on the color of the tepals. The inner staminodes are shorter and pure white or slightly off-white. Numerous seed heads enliven the plant right through summer and autumn. A plant that certainly earns its place in the garden.
Flowering season: mid to late spring.
Height: 6½ ft (2 m).
Zones: 3–9.

Quite a number of macropetala hybrids are available to gardeners. Seek and find a few choice ones.

Clematis macropetala 'Markham's Pink'

Of Earnest Markham fame, this is a beautiful variety. Flowers: sumptuous double, deep pink. In the author's garden it partners an autumn-flowering cherry, *Prunus x subhirtella* 'Autumnalis.'
Flowering season: early to late spring. Height: 10 ft (3 m).
Zones: 3–9.

Clematis macropetala 'Jan Lindmark'

From Sweden. Flowers: mauve pink-purple with slightly twisted outer tepals. The inner layer staminodes are narrower than the outer ones.
Flowering season: early to late spring.
Height: 8 ft (2.5 m).
Zones: 3–9.

Above:
Clematis macropetala.

Right:
***Clematis macropetala* 'Markham's Pink.'**

Left:
***Clematis macropetala* 'Blue Bird.'**

Clematis macropetala 'White Moth'

Of all the alpinas and macropetalas, this is the latest to come into flower. It is a delightful and not too vigorous plant with sea-green foliage. It grows through *Crinodendron hookerianum* (Lantern tree) in the author's small garden. The red flowers of the Lantern tree always look supremely good with the white flowers of 'White Moth.'
Flowering season: late spring to early summer.
Height: 6½ ft (2 m).
Zones: 3–9.

Montana Hybrids
(Pruning Group 1)

We have to thank Lady Amherst for introducing the montanas to British gardeners from North India. Almost every garden boasts a montana. However, montanas left to grow in gay abandon may prove to be an utter nuisance. Gardeners who grow montanas have to be diligent pruners. Once a montana is well-established, all new masses of growths should be removed immediately after flowering. Otherwise montanas will engulf every plant in their proximity. Various books advise gardeners to grow montanas over unsightly sheds, outhouses, or other eyesores in the garden. However, if a montana is carefully positioned in the garden and not allowed to run amok, it can be a delightful plant, in flower during late spring and early summer. What is more, quite a number of montanas bear scented flowers. When grown to cover unsightly objects, the enormous amount of intertwined growths of stems also become hiding places for all the snails in the world! Therefore, it is judicious to keep montanas under check, particularly in urban gardens where space may be at a premium. If space is not in question, then let the montanas exercise their freedom of growth and delight you with their flowers. I believe all gardeners should try to grow montanas as ground cover plants, provided there is ample space in their gardens. Propagation from cuttings and layering is recommended.

Although montanas are easy to grow and propagate from semi-ripe cuttings, they are not fully hardy, particularly in very cold climes. In parts of Britain, Ireland, and the US which are prone to late severe frosts, the buds and flowers of montanas can be severly damaged and look unsightly.

If growing montanas through large trees or conifers, it is important to choose robust ones so that they will be able to withstand the strain and stress of supporting the clematis. Keep montanas well away from shrubs—they will be strangled by the vigor of the clematis.

There are a number of montana hybrids available to gardeners, notably C. 'Tetrarose,' C. 'Freda,' C. 'Mayleen,' and C. 'Marjorie.' Some of the newcomers have proved to be welcome additions to the hybrids already well and truly established.

Left: *Clematis montana* 'Tetrarose.'

Right: *Clematis montana* 'Marjorie.'

Opposite: *Clematis montana* var. *rubens.*

Clematis montana 'Broughton Star' 1988

Leaves: bronze changing to green as they mature. Flowers: semi-double to fully double, cup-shaped, plum-pink. Grow this plant horizontally along a rope or a chain by training and tying the stems in so as to enjoy the unusual flowers.
Flowering season: late spring to early summer.
Height: 20–30 ft (6–9 m).
Zones: 7–9.

Clematis montana 'Warwickshire Rose' 1990s

Leaves: deep reddish bronze. Flowers: rose-pink. The foliage alone makes this plant worth growing and the flowers form a beautiful contrast.
Flowering season: late spring to early summer.
Height: 20–30 ft (6–9 m).
Zones: 7–9.

Double and Semi-Double Hybrids

While some gardeners prefer small single dainty blooms of clematis, there are many who are spellbound by the spectacular double and semi-double flowers of some specially bred hybrids. Almost all of them produce their double or semi-double flowers during late spring and early summer and bring further delight with another display of single flowers in early autumn. Occasionally, single, semi-double, and double flowers may be displayed at the same time, as in *Clematis* 'Louise Rowe,' or double flowers may be the rule throughout the flowering period as in the recently introduced hybrid, *C.* 'Josephine.' Double or semi-double flowers are borne on old wood made during the previous year and, therefore, these clematis should not be pruned. Should the plants need proper thinning or outgrow their allocated space after a number of years, as with other early-flowering species and hybrids, do not be afraid to remove a quantity of the old stems immediately after the first flush of flowers have come and gone.

These clematis can either be grown through other shrubs, climbing plants, or on their own. Ensure that the living support does not require any pruning before partnering a double-flowered clematis with it. Some varieties, especially the compact ones, will grow and flower well in large containers, provided they are well-nourished and thoroughly watered on a regular basis. The same procedures of course apply to plants growing in the open ground.

Most of these double-flowering hybrids prefer some sunshine; south-, east-, or west-facing aspects are ideal to ripen their wood and encourage flowering. If there is not enough light the flowers tend to open green, although the tepals will color as more light becomes available. Double-flowering hybrids may not give of their best, particularly during late spring, if the weather is cold and light levels are low.

Generally these plants are hardy in most parts of the British Isles. However, in severely cold areas, old growths from the previous season will not survive and, therefore, there will be no early flowers. As new growths appear with the onset of warm weather, flower buds will develop to open during mid to late summer and early autumn. Container-grown plants could be given protection from severe frost to save the old wood and help them to flower in late spring or early summer. Propagate from cuttings.

Clematis 'Daniel Deronda' is a very old variety which boasts semi-double and single flowers as well as spectacular and rather novel seed heads.

Clematis 'Arctic Queen' (PBR) 1994

This Evison/Poulson hybrid is a prolific flowerer, its special merit being that early and late flowers are fully-double, borne on old and new growths, respectively. Each creamy white flower measures 4–7 in. (10–18 cm) across.
Flowering season: late spring to early summer and early autumn.
Height: 10 ft (3 m). Suitable for growing in large containers.
Zones: 4–9.

Clematis 'Daniel Deronda' 1882

Charles Noble of Sunningdale Nurseries introduced this variety more than a century ago. The gentle twist and knot at the top of the spherical seed heads is novel and very attractive. Early summer flowers are semi-double, while the mid-summer to autumn ones are single. Both measure 7–8 in. (18–20 cm) across and have deep violet-blue tepals.
Flowering season: early summer to mid-autumn.
Height: 8–10 ft (2.5–3 m).
Zones: 4–9.

Clematis 'Josephine' (PBR) 1998

Both the early and late flowers of this Evison/Poulson cultivar are sumptuously double. Tepals are mauve-pink and pointed at the tips. The plant requires full sun to produce a number of vibrantly colored flowers; when given a position in the shade there will be fewer flowers and the tepals will be green.

Flowering season: early summer to early autumn.

Height: 5¾–8 ft (1.8–2.5 m). Suitable for growing in large containers.

Zones: 4–9.

Clematis 'Mrs James Mason' 1984

Raised and introduced by Barry Fretwell, this vigorous hybrid has a good pedigree—it is a cross between C. 'Vyvyan Pennel' and C. 'Dr Ruppel.' The early, large violet-blue double flowers have almost boat-shaped tepals, elegantly frilled and wavy at the edges. Single flowers are produced in great profusion in early autumn. The plant demands generous nourishment to show off its beautifully colored flowers.

Flowering season: late spring to early summer and early autumn.

Height: 5¾–10 ft (1.8–3 m).

Zones: 4–9.

Clematis 'Jackmanii Alba' 1877

Charles Noble of Sunningdale Nurseries is responsible for this hybrid. It is not a prolific flowerer but is a trouble-free plant that the newcomer to double-flowered clematis can grow with confidence. The first flush of flowers, with loose layers of pointed white tepals that appear to be washed with gentle blue and greenish dye, look attractive, but the early autumn single bluey white flowers have character and structure. This very vigorous plant of good constitution is not fussy about where it grows and may even tolerate a certain amount of wind.

Flowering season: early summer to early atumn.

Height: 10–13 ft (3–4 m).

Zones: 4–9.

Clematis 'Artic Queen' is a compact cultivar that requires no pruning.

Clematis 'Mrs George Jackman' 1877

This delightful hybrid from Jackman's of Woking produces semi-double flowers with creamy white overlapping tepals in late spring and early summer that are perfect in form and shape. An abundance of single flowers, which appear during mid to late summer, are a joy to behold.

Flowering season: late spring to early autumn. Suitable for container culture.

Height: 5¾–8 ft (1.8–2.5 m).

Zones: 4–9.

Clematis 'Sylvia Denny' 1983

Denny's of Preston raised this plant, which was introduced by Raymond Evison at Chelsea. The small to medium-sized semi-double pure white flowers of 'Sylvia Denny' will appeal to all camellia fans. Unlike the flowers of 'Duchess of Edinburgh,' there is no trace of green in the tepals.

Flowering season: late spring to early summer and late summer to early autumn.

Height: 8–10 ft (2.5–3 m).

Zones: 4–9.

Large-Flowered Hybrids

The large-flowered hybrids are notable for their astounding range of colors and the sheer size of their flowers. The wealth of colors encompasses pinks, reds, purples, blues, and whites. Even the whites come in many shades. Large-flowered hybrids require more care and attention and are more prone to clematis wilt than the small-flowered species and hybrids. Patience is the name of the game and, invariably, as the plants settle down and get stronger they will reward the gardener with superb floral displays. Do not expect instant success with these hybrids. Some are easier than others. Give three growing seasons for the new plants to establish a strong and healthy root system, throw up new shoots from beneath the soil, and flower well. These hybrids need time to "creep, crawl, and leap." The aim should be to get the newly purchased plants to produce as many stems as possible by careful planting, regular mulching, watering, feeding, and pruning. Even with all the care given, some hybrids may refuse to cooperate with the gardener and may not perform well. Some may even sit and sulk. The cardinal rule is, "do not despair," or give up growing these magical plants. They are full of surprises!

With the exception of some varieties, it pays to grow large-flowered hybrids in association with other suitable garden plants. It is also helpful to have a basic knowledge of the differing pruning requirements of these large-flowered hybrids in choosing the right plants for the right positions in the garden. If in doubt, ask for advice about the plants and their requirements at a nursery before parting with your cash. Numerous named large-flowered hybrids are offered for sale in nurseries and garden centers. That does not mean all of them are top of the class in quality or carry the correct labels! So beware.

Propagation from cuttings is recommended. Plants grown from seed do not come true.

Early Large-Flowered Hybrids (Pruning Group 2)

Since these hybrids come into flower during late spring or early summer, they must not be pruned severely. They flower on old and new growths. Some may even flower again during late summer and early autumn, while a few may flower right through the growing season. A certain amount of tidying up of the plant may be undertaken immediately after the old stems have flowered. However, apart from removing dead and weak stems, refrain from dead-heading because some hybrids produce exquisite seed heads. What may appear to be young shaggy seed heads at the beginning will end up as beautifully groomed mature ones. It is as if a secret hairdresser is at work on these seed heads from the time they develop until the exquisite job is accomplished!

On the whole these hybrids are hardy. Should the old growths succumb to severe winters, the flowering season will be delayed. The plant will have to produce new shoots during spring to flower, and this may take anything from four to six weeks, or even more. Remove all the dead old stems, mulch, and feed the plants for an effective show of flowers.

Clematis 'Anna' 1974

This Swedish hybrid, raised by Magnus Johnson and named after his granddaughter, is a compact and free-flowering plant. The pearly pink flowers are fully rounded and composed of 6–8 tepals. The anthers are red. A sunny position produces the best performance.
Flowering season: late spring to early summer and early autumn.
Height: 5¾–8 ft (1.8-2.5m).
Zones: 4–9.

Clematis 'Anna Louise' (PBR) 1993

The violet-purple flowers of this Raymond Evison hybrid, named after his daughter, are produced freely. There is a central boss of delicate, reddish brown anthers amid the 6–8 tepals.
Flowering season: late spring to early summer and early autumn.
Height: 5¾–8 ft (1.8-2.5m).
Zones: 4–9.

Clematis 'Barbara Jackman'
1952

Raised by Rowland Jackman, of Jackman's of Woking fame, and named after his wife, this clematis should be given a north or northwest aspect for best coloring of the mauve-plum flowers. If planted in strong sunlight the flowers will fade. The anthers are cream-yellow. There are 6–8 tepals. The plant is a vigorous and bushy.
Flowering season: late spring to early summer and early autumn.
Height: 8–10 ft (2.5–3 m).
Zones: 4–9.

Clematis 'Bees' Jubilee'
1958

This Bees of Chester hybrid, named to commemorate the company's silver anniversary, resembles the tried, tested, and much enjoyed C. 'Nelly Moser.' Its mauvish pink flowers, which have 6–8 tepals, appear in great profusion. The anthers are light brown. The plant takes a while to settle down, but patience will pay handsome dividends. It prefers a good planting position and good feed.
Flowering season: late spring to early summer and early autumn.
Height: 5¾–8 ft (1.8–2.5 m).
Zones: 4–9.

Above right: Beautiful plum-pink flowers of *Clematis* 'Betty Risdon' are freely borne on a compact plant.

Below: Do not plant *Clematis* 'Caroline' in an area with strong sunshine. This will prevent the color of the flower from fading.

Clematis 'Betty Risdon'
1996

Raised by Vince and Sylvia Denny of Preston and named after the former treasurer of the British Clematis Society, this compact hybrid is a free-flowering plant. The flowers are plum-pink
Flowering season: late spring to early summer and early autumn.
Height: 5¾–8 ft (1.8–2.5 m).
Zones: 4–9.

Clematis 'Caroline'
1990s

Raised by Barry Fretwell, this is one of my favorites and quite popular with gardeners. A neat, tidy, and compact grower, it boasts beautiful pale pink, not very large flowers, 4 in. (10 cm) across, over a long flowering period. They have 6–8 tepals. The anthers are pale yellow. Plant in a position out of strong sunshine so that the flowers do not fade.

Flowering season: late spring to early summer and early autumn.
Height: 6½–8 ft (2–2.5 m). Suitable for growing in containers.
Zones: 4–9.

Clematis 'Corona'
1972

Raised in Sweden by Tage Lundell, this is a compact plant. Purple pinkish red flowers are borne in great profusion during the first flowering, fewer and somewhat paler ones in the second flowering season. They have 6–8 tepals. The anthers are dark red.
Flowering season: late spring to early summer and late summer to early autumn.
Height: 4–5¾ ft (1.2–1.8 m). Suitable for growing in containers.
Zones: 4–9.

Clematis 'Dawn'
1969

This Swedish hybrid, raised by Tage Lundell, is not a vigorous plant but is a good flowerer. Off-whitish pink flowers are produced freely and complement the young bronze spring foliage. The blunt, almost round, tepals (6–8) compose an appealingly shaped flower. The anthers are reddish brown. Having planted 'Dawn' in a sunny site, I had to move it to a position out of the sun because the flowers failed to retain their rather delightful coloring. Now, it brings color to my winter-flowering *Sarcococca humilis*. I recommend that 'Dawn' be grown through another low-growing shrub for an effective display. It is very frost hardy.

Flowering season: late spring to early summer occasionally in early autumn.

Height: 5¾ ft (1.8 m).

Zones: 4–9.

Right: Once she settles down in the garden you can count on *Clematis* 'Marie Boisselot' for a wonderful display of large white satiny flowers over a long period of time.

Below: *Clematis* 'General Sikorski' is a welcome Polish cultivar. The numerous mid-blue flowers carry a hint of red. Easy to grow.

Clematis 'Edith'
1974

Raised and introduced by Raymond Evison of Guernsey and named in honor of his mother, this clematis is a chance seedling from C. 'Mrs. Cholmondleley.' It is a compact plant with white flowers and prominent green bars on the tepals, of which there are 6–8. The anthers are dark red. 'Edith' has a long flowering period.

Flowering season: late spring to early autmn.

Height: 8–10 ft (2.5–3 m).

Zones: 4–9.

Clematis 'Fair Rosamond'
1871

A hybrid from Jackman's of Woking, 'Fair Rosamond' is a winner with the author. It performs exceptionally well year after year, even after being ruthlessly cut back one year to tidy up ten years of vigorous growth. While it flowers very freely, warm spring sunshine will enhance the color of the flowers and prompt them to exude some scent. It tends to sulk a bit in cold weather and the tepals do not open out satisfactorily. The creamy white flowers boast a beautiful shape with 6–8 fine pointed tepals. The anthers are dark purple-red. Any but a shady aspect will suit it.

Flowering season: late spring to early summer and intermittently in late summer to early autumn.

Height: 8 ft (2.5 m).

Zones: 4–9.

Clematis 'General Sikorski' 1980

This excellent Polish hybrid, raised by Wladyslaw Noll and introduced by Jim Fisk, is of strong constitution, quick to establish itself, and flower freely. Newcomers to clematis will have no problem with 'General Sikorski'. With a hint of red in their six mid-blue broad rounded and finely scalloped tepals, the flowers look rich. The anthers are yellow. Although some authors advise that this clematis can be grown in association with shrubs and roses, in the author's garden 'General Sikorski' failed to perform satisfactorily when grown with other plants. Given a place all on its own, the plant took off to yield an abundance of flowers over a long period.
Flowering season: early to late summer.
Height: 8–10 ft (2.5–3 m).
Zones: 4–9.

Clematis 'Helen Cropper' 1985

Raised by Vince and Sylvia Denny of Preston, 'Helen Cropper' is a splendid plant with neat foliage and eye-catching flowers. The large dusky pinkish mauve flowers make a lasting impression with their eight wavy-to-crinkly edged, overlapping tepals. The anthers are red. This clematis is well worth a place in any garden.
Flowering season: late spring to early summer and late summer to early autumn.
Height: 8–10 ft (2.5–3 m).
Zones: 4–9.

Clematis 'Fujimusume' is a first class plant, ideal for growing in large containers. It has glossy green foliage and elegant wedgewood-blue, velvety smooth flowers.

Clematis 'Fujimusume' 1952

Sejurn Arai raised this magnificent Japanese hybrid that is the author's firm favorite. It is a neat, tidy, and strong grower with handsome dark green foliage. The delightful wedgewood-blue early velvety smooth flowers, with six to eight tepals, measure 6–8 in. (15–18 cm) across and are borne freely. The flower stalks are long and strong, enabling the flowers to be held well in position. The anthers are golden yellow and the seed heads gold and extremely beautiful. The plant is highly recommended for container culture. Give it a north-facing aspect. Although this is an early-flowering hybrid, it can be pruned hard. It is essential to feed it well.
Flowering season: early to late summer.
Height: 5¾ ft (1.8 m).
Zones: 4–9.

Clematis 'Ken Donson' 1976

Beautiful foliage, as well as deep blue well-shaped flowers, with six to eight tepals, characterize this Pennells of Lincoln hybrid. The anthers are golden yellow. However, the author grows this clematis just for its spherical seed heads—they are simply perfect.
Flowering season: early summer to early autumn.
Height: 8–12 ft (2.5-3.6m)
Zones: 4–9.

Clematis 'Marie Boisselot' (syn. 'Mme. le Coultre') 1885

Raised by Auguste Boisselot, this French hybrid must be the best-known, most widely grown, loved, and discussed of all the white-flowered clematis. The name itself has become an enigma. Pure white, satiny, and eight-tepalled flowers with a central crown of creamy white stamens, though not held upright by the stalks, are an absolute joy. The anthers are golden yellow. It is very vigorous plant but, from the author's experience, the flowers are not produced in great profusion and do not smother it. It is a good idea not to let the stems climb too high but to bend them gently and train them to grow horizontally just to admire the shape, size, sheer beauty, and whiteness of madame's flowers. I recommend that this clematis be trained through other low-growing shrubs. It may be pruned hard early in the year though there will be a loss of early flowers. Wait patiently for her early autumn show.
Flowering season: early summer to early autumn.
Height: 8–12 ft (2.5–3.6 m); known to grow much higher in some gardens.
Zones: 4–9.

Clematis 'Miss Bateman'
1869

Raised by Charles Noble of Sunningdale 'Miss Bateman' boasts elegant white flowers. Growing through the spring-flowering *Magnolia stellata* in the author's small garden, the slightly satiny flowers with each of the six to eight tepals clearly marked with a green prominent stripe, look exceptionally good during early spring. The anthers are reddish brown. This clematis flowers very freely and seems to enjoy producing an abundance of new shoots every year. Remove some of the stems each year after flowering, once the plant is well established. 'Miss Bateman' will grow happily anywhere in the garden, although it can be grown in a large container.
Flowering season: mid-spring to early summer. (In the author's garden it flowers from early spring to early summer.)
Height: 5¾–8 ft (1.8–2.5 m).
Zones: 4–9.

Clematis 'Mrs N. Thompson'
1961

This popular Pennells of Lincoln hybrid has vibrant violet-purple flowers. The red bar which runs along the center of each of the four to six tepals is an attractive feature, and the young flowers have a velvety sheen. The anthers are dark red. It is a compact plant, though not full of vigor. Try growing it through a low-growing *Spirea japonica* 'Goldflame.'
Flowering season: late spring to early summer and early autumn.
Height: 5¾–8 ft (1.8–2.5 m).
Zones: 4–9.

Clematis 'Niobe'
1975

Which garden would be without this Polish hybrid? Raised by Wladyslaw Noll and introduced by Jim Fisk, 'Niobe,' provided it is the genuine article, takes a while to settle down, grow strong, learn to grow out of clematis wilt, and then ventures out to delight the gardener. It is not a vigorous, bushy plant, but the sheer beauty of the juvenile flowers as they open and expose the five to six crushed velvet tepals, bordering on an almost ruby reddish black, is a sight not to be missed. The anthers are yellow. It is a shame that the older

Right: *Clematis* 'Miss Bateman' is a good scrambler that is happy among other garden plants. Its satiny white flowers contrast with reddish brown anthers from late spring onward.

Opposite: *Clematis* 'Niobe' has flowers with crushed velvet, almost ruby-reddish black tepals which make for an impressive show over a long period of time. A compact plant recommended for short-term pot culture but refrain from growing through other stronger growing plants in the garden.

flowers fade badly, the tepals making an ugly exit, but the author recommends this clematis very highly. Be patient with 'Niobe.' Give the plant at least three seasons of growth and grow it on its own, preferably in an elegant container and site it in a sunny spot. It seldom needs major pruning.
Flowering season: late spring to early autumn.
Height: 4–5¾ ft (1.2–1.8 m).
Zones: .4–9.

Clematis 'Richard Pennell'
1974

The magical and unusual crown of stamens, which seem to have undergone a rotation or a twirl and remained in that position, is sufficient reason for growing this Pennells of Lincoln hybrid. It is a marvelous, vigorous plant with dark pinkish lavender, full

flowers measuring nearly 8 in. (20 cm) across. They have six to eight tepals. The anthers are golden.
Flowering season: late spring to early summer and early autumn.
Height: 8–10 ft (2.5–3 m).
Zones: 4–9.

Clematis 'Ruby Glow'
1975

A Jim Fisk introduction, this plant has come back into popularity. It is a very free-flowering clematis and has large, glowing rosy purple flowers with six to eight tepals. The anthers are red.
Flowering season: early summer to early autumn.
Height: 8–12 ft (2.5–3.6 m).
Zones: 4–9.

Clematis 'Royal Velvet' (PBR) 1993

This Evison/Poulsen hybrid distinguishes itself with reddish purple, rich velvety flowers, which are very freely produced from late spring to early fall. The lightly ridged margins of the six to eight tepals carry a purple-red bar. The young bronze foliage is a further attraction. The anthers are deep red.
Flowering season: late
spring to early summer
and late summer to early
autumn.
Height: 5¾–8 ft (1.8–
2.5 m).
Zones: 4–9.

Clematis 'Sealand Gem' 1957

Bees of Chester named this hybrid after their Sealand Nursery. It grows through *Viburnum tinus* 'Gwenllian,' and flowers exceptionally well, in the author's garden. The delightful, not very large, lavender-blue flowers with eight slightly crinkled tepals, do not open wide but become somewhat twisted to make the entire flower appear fuller. The flower color tends to fade in strong sun. The anthers are reddish brown.
Flowering season: late
spring to early summer
and early autumn.
Height: 10 ft (3 m).
Zones: 4–9.

Brighten a dark corner with *Clematis* 'Silver Moon.' Its fine silvery mauvish gray flowers with a crown of creamy yellow stamens make for a handsome display.

Clematis 'Silver Moon' 1971

Raised by Percy Picton and introduced by Jim Fisk, the name of this hybrid matches the color and texture of its flowers. Brighten a dark corner with 'Silver Moon.' Be sure to grow through a low-growing shrub with dark green foliage. Numerous late spring and early summer buds burst open to display silvery mauvish gray, almost star-shaped, fine and full flowers with a delicate satiny sheen. The six to eight wide and blunt round tepals with slightly crinkled margins, particularly in mature flowers, and the crown of creamy yellow stamens, make for a handsome display. The anthers are creamy yellow.
Flowering season: late
spring to early autumn.
Height: 8–10 ft (2.5–3 m).
Zones: 4–9.

Clematis 'Sunset' 1980s

This American hybrid, raised by Steffens Clematis Nursery, is an ideal plant for a very wide and deep terra-cotta pot. However, when grown in a pot it should be top-dressed annually and fed regularly during the growing season to enable it to flower well. Delightful purple-reddish pink flowers, measuring only about 1½ in. (4 cm) across, are freely produced. They have six tepals. The anthers are creamy yellow.
Flowering season: late
spring to early autumn.
Height: 8 ft (2.5 m).
Zones: 4–9.

Clematis 'William Kennett' 1875

Raised by Mr. H. Cobbet of Surrey, 'William Kennett' is an easy, trouble-free clematis that should be in every beginner's clematis collection. Rich lavender-blue flowers, measuring about 6 in. (15 cm) across, are produced in great profusion from late spring onwards. Fully opened flowers with six neatly overlapping, broad and wavy-edged tepals, gently tapering to short points and the striking dark maroonish red anthers are welcome features of this very old hybrid. It is a vigorous plant that needs space to grow well and show off its flowers and heart-shaped foliage. If necessary and if space is limited, tidy and prune the plant back hard early in the year and the new growths will furnish plenty of flowers. The author has seen this clematis partnered with *Rosa xanthina* 'Canary Bird.' If the gardener does not wish to be attacked by the thorns of the rose, choose a golden leaved Mexican orange blossom, such as *Choisya ternata* 'Sundance,' as a partner instead and make 'William Kennet' enjoy his life in the garden.
Flowering season: late
spring to early autumn.
Height: 10–14¾ ft (3–
4.5 m).
Zones: 4–9.

Mid-Season and Late Large-Flowered Hybrids

(Pruning Group 3: where there are exceptions to the rule for this group of pruning hard in late winter to early spring, instructions accompany the notes on individual clematis.)

Clematis 'Ascotiensis'
1874

Raised by John Standish, this hybrid takes its time to settle down and establish itself. However, here is a clematis, though a late-flowering variety, which may come into flower in mid-summer, thus continuing the drama and rhythm created by the late spring/early summer-flowering clematis in the garden. It is a vigorous plant that may be grown on its own or, preferably, through a climbing *Rosa* 'Golden Showers' or a shrub, such as gold-leaved spirea. The well-formed, no-fuss flowers are lavender-blue with four to six broad wavy tepals, narrowing to pointed tips. The anthers are creamish beige.
Flowering season: mid-summer to early autumn.
Height: 10–12 ft (3–3.6 m).
Zones: 3–9.

Right: The flowers of *Clematis* 'Comtesse de Bouchaud' are borne in great profusion. The pink hue combines comfortably with other clematis varieties.

Below: *Clematis* 'Ascotiensis.' A vigorous climber with well formed no-fuss lavender-blue flowers. Associates well with climbing roses and shrubs.

Clematis 'Comtesse de Bouchaud'
1903

Raised by Morel in France, this age-old clematis is fairly well-known to most gardeners. In Monet's garden in Giverny, France, it grows and produces flowers in great profusion against a handsome sunny wall. It is an ideal companion for the silver-gray leaved Californian poppy, *Romneya coulteri*. The flowers are truly pink and boast a wonderful satiny sheen. The six to eight broad, rounded tepals are crinkled along the margins. The furrows and indentations along the midribs and veins of the tepals confer additional structure upon them. The anthers are cream. 'Comtesse de Bouchaud' is a tried and true hybrid, easy to grow, does not climb to great heights, and is not prone to clematis wilt. It is an ideal clematis for gardeners with restricted space.
Flowering season: mid to late summer.
Height: 5¾–10 ft (1.8–3 m).
Zones: 4–9.

Clematis 'Gipsy Queen'
1877

Raised by Cripps & Sons of Tunbridge Wells, England, the velvety plum-purple flowers are mistaken for those of *Clematis* 'Jackmanii.' The difference is that the wider tepals (six) of the 'Gipsy Queen' narrow distinctly toward the base. The anthers are dark red. The plant flowers on both old and new wood, although it pays to prune the former hard to allow the plant to put on an excellent display later in the season. Treat it as a member of pruning group 3 to enjoy a long period of delightful flowers. In the author's garden, 'Perle d'Azur' and 'Gipsy Queen' share a free-standing trellis beside the rose 'Canary Bird' and both find their way into its arching branches. The three-way partnership works admirably.
Flowering season: mid-summer to early autumn.
Height: 10–12 ft (3–3.6 m).
Zones: 3–9.

Clematis 'Jackmanii Superba'
1878

The flowers of this Jackman of Woking hybrid are rich purple with a reddish tint, though fading with age. The four broad, almost square, tepals make the flowers look somewhat larger than those of the ubiquitous—and deservedly popular—'Jackmanii'. The anthers are beige. Propagate from cuttings, although it is not easy.
Flowering season: mid to late summer.
Height: 8–10 ft (2.5–3 m).
Zones: 3–9.

Clematis 'John Huxtable'
1967

Named after the gentleman who raised the plant, which is a chance seedling of 'Comtesse de Bouchaud.' The creamy white flowers may be described as the white counterparts of the mother plant. They have four to six tepals. The anthers are yellow. The plant is vigorous in its habit and rewards the gardener with an abundance of blooms.
Flowering season: mid to late summer.
Height: 5¾–8 ft (1.8–2.5 m).
Zones: 3–9.

Clematis 'Lady Betty Balfour'
1910

A plant that was sold to the author as *Clematis* 'Victoria' turned out to be 'Lady Betty Balfour.' Raised by Jackman's of Woking, this plant is only for warm, sunny, autumnal gardens not subjected to early frost. As a very late flowerer, it requires a south-facing aspect so that

Right: The very rich purple colored flowers of *Clematis* 'Jackmanii Superba' are a joy from midsummer onward.

Below: *Clematis* 'John Huxtable'. The elegantly shaped creamy-white flowers are bright and beautiful.

all the buds get an opportunity to open fully and exhibit the rich deep purple-blue flowers of six to eight tepals. The anthers are yellow. This extremely vigorous hybrid throws up numerous new shoots each year, and I would rate it as an excellent, trouble-free clematis, contrary to the belief that it is a martyr to clematis wilt. Severe pruning during late winter and early spring, heavy mulching with nutrients, water, and plenty of sunshine are all that the plant requires to flower well. I recommend that the top-flowered wood be cut back, if growing through another

strong shrub or small tree, during late autumn or early winter. Prune away all the remaining old growths later on, both for the sake of supporting the living host and the clematis. Otherwise, there will be masses of tangled old wood embedded in the branches of the shrub or small tree. The drama and movement created by 'Lady Betty Balfour' growing in close proximity to *Clematis* 'Helios' (see page 100) in the author's garden is just splendid!

Flowering season: early to mid-autumn.
Height: 11–14¾ ft (3.5– 4.5 m).
Zones: 3–9.

Clematis 'Perle d'Azur' 1885

A clear favorite with many gardeners, this is a French hybrid raised by Francisque Morel. It is grown to perfection in the gardens of Sissinghurst, England. Although it tends to wilt as a young plant, it will grow out of it—be patient—and grow away with vigor. The lovely light blue flowers show a hint of pinkish red tint at the base of their 4–6 rounded tepals that have recurving tips. The anthers are light yellow. The collective effect of these slightly nodding flowers ascending through, up, and over a strong conifer, *Abies koreana*, and cascading down is truly a spectacular sight. The only slight drawback is a proneness to mildew. Try partnering this clematis with one of the following climbing roses: 'School

Girl,' 'Mermaid,' or 'Golden Showers.' Propagation is not easy.
Flowering season: early summer to early autumn.
Height: 10–11 ft (3–3.5 m).
Zones: 3–9.

Clematis 'Pink Fantasy' 1975

This is a good, compact and extremely floriferous Canadian hybrid introduced by Jim Fisk. Grow it in a large container or a chimney pot and let the flower-smothered stems cascade down, or grow it horizontally on a raised bed by pegging down the stems at intervals. It can even be grown through low-growing shrubs or groundcover roses. The young flowers are true shell pink in color and take on different hues from flower to flower and even tepal to tepal in the same flower. The color fades to whitish pink as the flowers mature. As the flowers open, some of the six tepals, which have slightly crimpled margins, twist and gradually open out flat, exposing the central stamens with reddish beige anthers. Although it is a very good patio plant, the color will fade in intense sunlight. A distinct advantage of growing this hybrid, as opposed to 'Hagley Hybrid,' is that the older lower leaves of 'Pink Fantasy' do not turn unsightly brown.
Flowering season: early summer to early fall.
Height: 6 ft (1.8 m).
Zones: 3–9.

Top: *Clematis* 'Perle d'Azur' is full of charm and beauty. The light blue slightly nodding flowers are borne in great profusion from summer to early autumn.

Above: *Clematis* 'Ville de Lyon' is a classic clematis which carries carmine red flowers from old to new wood. To prune or not to prune is the question.

Clematis 'Star of India' 1867

If only the stems and flowers can be maintained mildew-free, this hybrid, introduced by Cripps of Tunbridge Wells, England, is a star indeed. It is a moderately strong-growing plant that boasts numerous blooms over a long period of time. The young vibrant flowers are rich plum-purple in color with reddish purple central bars on the tepals, which vary in number from 4 to 6 from flower to flower. Try partnering this clematis with *Rosa* 'Compassion' or 'Handel.'
Flowering season: early summer to early fall.
Height: 10–12 ft (3– 3.6 m).
Zones: 3–9.

Clematis 'Ville de Lyon' 1899

A century old and deservedly popular, this vigorous French hybrid was raised by Morel, by all accounts an outstanding hybridizer. To prune or not to prune is a question that may arise with this plant, because 'Ville de Lyon' will produce flowers on the previous year's old wood early in the season, followed by an abundance of blooms from new growths. In the author's garden this plant shares a low wooden arch with *C. alpina* 'Willy' and the inevitable bare basal stems of both plants are well hidden from view by low to medium-sized growing shrubs on either side of the arch. Neither clematis is subjected to hard pruning. However, if it is grown on its own or through another early-flowering shrub, it may be hard-pruned but there will be no early flowers. The neat, rounded flowers are carmine-red and the six broad, distinctly veined tepals terminate in blunt tips. The anthers are yellow. Advisable not to let this clematis go thirsty or hungry early in the growing season to delay the browning of the leaves. It is a valuable garden plant.
Flowering season: late spring to early autumn, if not pruned or pruned very lightly; early summer to early autumn, if pruned hard.
Height: 10–12 ft (3–3.6 m) or more, depending on pruning (Group 2 or 3).
Zones: 3–9.

Viticella Species and Hybrids
(Pruning Group 3)

They may not be the largest or the most colorful of clematis but the *viticellas* are an excellent group of plants that can be grown with great ease and confidence, posing no problem to either novice or expert gardeners. Southern Europe is home to this group of clematis, also known as the purple Virgin's Bower. The species and hybrids are all deciduous, very hardy, full of vigor, floriferous, and can withstand a certain amount of wind exposure, unlike the large-flowered hybrids. Almost all are wilt-resistant. They flower on the current season's growths and should be pruned very hard earlier in the year for a spectacular display from mid-summer to early autumn, and even mid-autumn in mild maritime gardens. The flowers are small, usually nodding or semi-nodding.

They can be grown on their own on suitable supports, or through robust shrubs, small to medium trees, climbing roses or as ground cover plants. As these plants can become very vigorous it is essential to choose their living supports, partnering plants, very carefully to avoid any damage to the latter. Prune away all the top growths of those clematis growing on or over winter-flowering plants to allow the latter to show off their flowers. No harm will come to this group of clematis if pruning is undertaken during late autumn or early winter in localities which do not suffer from severe frost. Propagate from cuttings or layering.

Above: *Clematis viticella* 'Alba Luxurians'. A dash of green on the otherwise white tepals add a touch of the unusual to the flowers. A gift to flower arrangers.

Below: The bell-shaped and gently nodding flowers of *Clematis viticella* are borne either singly or in threes from the axils of new growths.

Clematis viticella
1569

A parent to all the viticella hybrids, the species in cultivation is variable. Plants offered for sale are often raised from seed, so it is advisable to buy this plant in flower. The bell-shaped four-tepalled flowers are normally rich mauve-purple, borne singly or in clusters.
Flowering season: mid-summer to early fall.
Height: 10–12 ft (3–3.6 m).
Zones: 3–9.

Clematis viticella
'Abundance'
Early 1900?

Considerable confusion abounds as to the identity of the hybridizer of this plant. Morel of France or Jackman of Woking? The gently nodding flowers are deep pink to red, the four to five tepals recurving at the margins and tips. The anthers are yellow.
Flowering season: mid-summer to early autumn.
Height: 10–12 ft (3–3.6 m).
Zones: 3–9.

Clematis viticella
'Alba Luxurians'
Circa 1900

"White tepals with a dash of bright green at the tips" is an apt description of the flowers of this clematis, raised by Veitch & Sons in England. Some gardeners may find the white-green coloring of the flowers very attractive while others may not. Flower arrangers are invariably thrilled to include them in their arrangements. The bell-like flowers, with four to five recurving tepals, measure about 3¼ in. (8 cm) across and open flat. They are produced in abundance. Let the sun shine upon the smartly veined and textured tepals. The anthers are purplish black.
Flowering season: mid-summer to early autumn.
Height: 10–12 ft (3–3.6 m).
Zones: 3–9.

Clematis viticella 'Betty Corning' 1932

Named after the American lady who spotted it on "an Albany side street," this hybrid tends not to flower profusely when young. The nodding, bell-shaped, pale lilac and faintly scented flowers are handsome. In mature flowers the four tepals recurve elegantly at the tips. The anthers are yellow. It is well worth growing this hybrid as a specimen plant. It grows against a west-facing wall in the author's garden with *Rosa* 'Graham Thomas' growing in front of it. The flowers of 'Betty Corning' coincide with those of the rose—a perfect combination.
Flowering season: early summer to early autumn.
Height: 8–10 ft (2.5–3 m).
Zones: 3–9.

Clematis viticella 'Etoile Violette' 1885

If there is one viticella hybrid the author would heartily recommend growing just for the sheer profusion and magical deep rich violet-purple of the flowers, it will have to be 'Etoile Violette.' It is yet another wonderful gift from Morel of France. Just plant this hybrid in close proximity to a gold-leaved large shrub and enjoy the spectacle. It grows in front of a 20-year-old *Acer Shiraswanum* 'Aureum' (Golden Full Moon Maple) in the author's garden. It will look equally good associated with a vigorous *Rosa* 'New Dawn.' The flowers measure 3¼–4 in. (8–10 cm) across and each has a conspicuous bunch of yellow stamens. The number of tepals varies (four to six). The

Above: The claret red flowers of *Clematis viticella* 'Madame Julia Correvon' are vibrant when the sun shines upon them. The slightly twisted buds are characteristic of this *viticella* cultivar.

Left: The sheer velvety smooth tepals of flowers borne in great profusion make *Clematis viticella* 'Etoile Violette.' A must for every garden.

anthers are yellow.
Flowering season: mid-summer to early autumn.
Height: 10–13 ft (3–4 m).
Zones: 3–9.

Clematis viticella 'Kermesina' 1883

This French hybrid, raised by Lemoine, is identified by a large white splotch at the base of each of the four tepals. The flowers are cheerful red in color and the stamens are dark reddish brown. The anthers are brownish black. It is a very vigorous plant, suitable for growing on a large strong shrub, golden conifer, climbing rose, or a medium-sized tree.
Flowering season: mid-summer to early autumn.
Height: 10–14¾ ft (3–4.5 m).
Zones: 3–9.

Clematis viticella 'Madame Julia Correvon' 1900

Raised by Morel in France, 'Mme Julia Correvon' grows well and flowers freely. The buds, which are narrow and slightly twisted at the tips, open gradually to reveal their young, claret-red flowers with a velvety sheen and contrasting yellow stamens. As the flowers mature, the four to six tepals recurve, twist, and become gappy but retain their color. The anthers are yellow. This is not especially vigorous plant, but may be grown in a container for an effective display on the patio. The flowers look vibrant when the sun shines upon them. The only drawback is that the older lower leaves tend to wither and brown. In the author's garden this clematis is planted behind an evergreen shrub, *Sarcococca hookeriana* var. *humilis*.
Flowering season: early summer to early autumn.
Height: about 10 ft (3 m).
Zones: 3–9.

Clematis viticella 'Pagoda'
Circa 1970

Gardeners should thank the late John Treasure of Burford House Gardens for this aptly named, captivating hybrid. When the flowers open fully the shape is just that—of a pagoda. This is a vigorous, floriferous plant. The distinctly veined four tepals are creamy pinkish mauve with a much deeper, similarly colored, central band on the outside. As the flowers mature, the tepals recurve and twist at the tips. This plant shares an obelisk with *C.* 'Niobe' (rich black-reddish flowers) in the author's garden.
Flowering season: early summer to early autumn.
Height: 8–10 ft (2.5–3 m).
Zones: 4–9.

Clematis viticella 'Polish Spirit'
1989

A vigorous Polish hybrid, raised by Brother Stefan Franczak and introduced to British gardeners by Raymond Evison, the foliage is smothered when this superb plant is in full flower. The entire plant is well furnished with its leaves and the older leaves do not wither and brown

as they do in some of the other viticellas. The deep purple flowers, with 5 or 6 tepals, have a satin sheen and a semi-nodding habit. The anthers are blackish red. This can be rated as a five-star clematis, which should be grown on its own on a suitable support or be given a strong climbing rose or a gold- or gray-leaved large shrub or a small tree as a partner.
Flowering season: mid-summer to early autumn.
Height: 10–13 ft (3–4 m).
Zones: 6–9.

Above: *Clematis viticella* 'Pagoda' is a vigorous plant with creamy pinkish mauve flowers full of character and texture.

Opposite: *Clematis viticella* 'Purpurea Plena Elegans.' Sometimes known as 'PPE,' the sumptuous double flowers of this very old European variety are produced in abundance over a long period.

Clematis viticella 'Purpurea Plena Elegans'
16th Century?

This very old viticella is probably a "sport" and has sumptuous double rosettes of dull magenta, sterile flowers. Some authors describe the color as violet-purple. The layers of reflexed tepals twist gently as the flowers mature. It is a vigorous plant and needs space to grow and flower well. In the author's garden, it shares a wooden arch with *C.* 'Huldine.'
Flowering season: mid-summer to early autumn.
Height: 10–14¾ ft (3–4.5 m).
Zones: 3–9.

Clematis viticella 'Royal Velours'
1914

Morel of France is credited with this hybrid. The rich, deep velvety reddish purple flowers are composed of four rounded tepals with body and texture. The anthers are greenish black. Site the plant carefully and in a reasonably sunny position. I suggest planting it in close proximity to *Pyrus salcifolia* 'Pendula' (Weeping Willow-Leaved Pear) and allowing the wandering stems of 'Royal Velours' to show off its blossoms against the gray leaves of its companion.
Flowering season: mid-summer to early autumn.
Height: 10–14¾ ft (3–4.5 m).
Zones: 3–9.

Clematis viticella 'Venosa Violacea'
1884

Raised by Lemoine in France, this hybrid is celebrated among the *viticellas* for its unusually large whitish purple flowers, measuring 4 in. (10 cm) across. The five or six recurved tepals are richly veined, and the purple color on a white background is more intense toward the margins. The anthers are blackish puple.
Flowering season: early summer to mid-autumn.
Height: 8–10 ft (2.5–3 m).
Zones: 3–9.

Texensis Species and Hybrids
(Pruning Group 3)

Clematis texensis is the only scarlet-flowered member of the genus *Clematis* known to grow in the wild. It hails from Texas, and any gardener who manages to get the true species (pure bright red flowers) and grow it successfully is very fortunate indeed. The late John Treasure of Burford House garden (Treasures of Tenbury) fame, named this clematis 'The Scarlet Lady.' The texensis hybrids, old and new, are exceedingly valuable plants, renowned for their beautifully shaped flowers, some nodding, and others resembling small tulips. The flowering period is generally from early summer to early autumn, some flowering earlier than others. They are semi-herbaceous scramblers by habit and may be grown very successfully in association with small to medium-sized shrubs. Ideally those hybrids which boast tulip-like flowers should be grown at eye level, so that it is possible to look down into the flowers. It is wisest to treat them like other garden perennials and prune away all the previous season's stems to ground level during late winter or early spring. Many new shoots will emerge from below ground level annually. From the author's experience, the heavier the mulch and the older the plant, the more these new shoots are produced. Unfortunately, the Texan hybrids are prone to mildew; this disease may be avoided by not planting the hybrids in dry sites or too close to walls and by choosing positions where there will be good air circulation through the plants. Avoid north-facing aspects. Early spraying with suitable fungicides may also help to combat the infection. Propagation, from cuttings, is not easy.

Left: *Clematis texensis* 'Duchess of Albany.' A vigorous Texan which should be grown away from valuable garden plants. Handsome, clear pink flowers are composed of fleshy tepals.

Below: The delicate, elegant, and beautiful cherry red flowers of *Clematis texensis* 'Etoile Rose' are simply magical.

Clematis texensis
(see page 115)

Clematis texensis 'Duchess of Albany'
1890

This Jackman's of Woking hybrid has an abundance of grayish green foliage and clear pink four-tepalled, upward-facing, long tulip-like flowers with pink anthers. The thick and fleshy tepals carry dark pink central bars. Give 'Duchess of Albany' a place away from valuable shrubs and perennials in the garden. She is vigorous!
Flowering season: midsummer to mid-autumn.
Height: 8–10 ft (2.5–3 m).
Zones: 3–9.

Clematis texensis 'Etoile Rose'
Circa 1903

An enchanting and vigorous hybrid, raised by Lemoine of France. The nodding, deep cherry-pink, four-tepalled flowers are produced in abundance over a lengthy flowering period. The tepals are thick and fleshy with saw-toothed, silvery pink edges and recurved tips. As the flowers mature they open fully, revealing the pale yellow anthers. Use grown-up and over-tall shrubs or small trees for support, so the color, form, and shape of the flowers can be admired fully.
Flowering season: midsummer to mid-autumn.
Height: 8–10 ft (2.5–3 m) or more.
Zones: 4–9.

Clematis texensis 'Sir Trevor Lawrence' 1890

A Jackmans of Woking hybrid rescued and brought back into wider cultivation by Christopher Lloyd. Named after a former president of the Royal Horticultural Society, London, the flowers are incandescent reddish pinkpurple with longitudinally veined tepals. The tepal tips recurve gently and fold over as the flowers mature to expose the creamy yellow stamens. Plant in a site where sunlight and shade can play upon the color of the flowers.

Flowering season: midsummer to mid-autumn.
Height: 8–10 ft (2.5–3 m).
Zones: 4–9.

Clematis texensis 'Gravetye Beauty' 1914

Raised by Morel of France and named and introduced by William Robinson of Gravetye Manor-fame, this not very vigorous hybrid's rich ruby-red, young tulip-like flowers with a satin sheen are delightful. As the flowers mature they assume an open star shape, when the reddish brown anthers can be seen fully. The tepals vary between 4 and 6. The plant is best trained along the ground and allowed to scramble through other low-growing herbaceous perennials. In mild maritime gardens, flowering starts as early as late spring or early summer if the previous year's stems are not pruned.

Flowering season: mid to late summer.
Height: 5¾–8 ft (1.8–2.5 m).
Zones: 4–9.

Clematis texensis 'Princess Diana' 1984

Called 'The Princess of Wales' until recently, this gem of a plant was raised by Barry Fretwell. In the hybridizer's own words, the trumpet-shaped flowers are "vibrant pink having a luminous quality to be seen rather than described. A further asset is that this deep pink extends to the outside of the sepals, further complemented by a prominent tuft of creamy yellow stamens."

Flowering season: mid-summer to mid- autumn.
Height: 5¾–8 ft (1.8–2.5 m).
Zones: 4–9.

Above: The rich ruby red young tulip-shaped flowers of *Clematis texensis* 'Gravetye Beauty' are welcome additions in any herbaceous border from mid to late summer.

Right: *Clematis texensis* 'Princess Diana' is a very popular hybrid noted for its luminous pink flowers. Associates well with many medium sized shrubs in the garden.

Tangutica Species and Hybrids
(Pruning Group 3 unless otherwise stated)

Gardeners are still waiting for a true yellow large-flowered hybrid and, who knows, some genius of a hybridizer may just make that dream come true one day. For the time being we have to be content with the yellow-flowered tanguticas and their hybrids. With regard to pruning, hard-prune one half of the old stems (the previous year's growths) to ground level and leave the other half to come into flower during early summer or do not prune at all if the clematis is growing up and over large shrubs or small trees. Some of the plants listed below are quite vigorous. Be careful where you site them if garden space is at a premium.

Clematis tangutica 'Aureolin'
Circa 1979

A Dutch hybrid raised at the Boskoop Research Station in Holland, the lemon-yellow pendent flowers are slightly larger than those of the ubiquitous vigorous tangutica species. They open wide and are followed by handsome seed heads.
Flowering season: mid-summer to mid-autumn.
Height: 8–10 ft (2.5–3 m).
Zones: 4–9.

Clematis tangutica 'Bill Mackenzie'
1968

This is a seedling selected by Bill Mackenzie at the Waterperry Horticultural College gardens in Oxfordshire, England. Waxy yellow, wide open flowers, composed of four thick fleshy tepals, are borne in great profusion on a fine vigorous plant. The tepals taper toward gently upturned pointed tips. The central mass of reddish brown filaments and browny yellow anthers contrast beautifully with golden yellow tepals. Large silvery seed heads intermingle with the flowers over a long flowering period. This clematis is highly recommended. Planted at a short distance from *Sorbus acuparia* 'Joseph Rock' in the author's garden, bil-

Above: *Clematis tangutica* 'Helios' is a star plant noted for its long flowering period. It carries its bright yellow flowers and silky seed heads from early summer onward if not hard pruned.

Left: *Clematis tangutica.* Copy its growth pattern in its native habitat and grow this species to form mounds of foliage and small lantern-like flowers.

lowing green stems of 'Bill Mackenzie' climb up and over the branches of the tree with great ease and bring mid-summer color to it. Avoid seed-raised plants.
Flowering season: early summer to mid-autumn.
Height: 20–25 ft (6–7.5m).
Zones: 4–9.

Clematis tangutica 'Helios'
1988

This excellent, disease-free, modestly vigorous plant, raised by the Boskoop Experimental Station in Holland, is just the one for gardens with restricted spaces. In the author's garden it commences flowering as early as late spring and continues until mid-autumn. The gently nodding flowers with bright yellow tepals open quite flat, with the pointed tips reflexing like a Turk's cap. The open flower varies in diameter from 2½–3½ in. (6.5–9 cm). The foliage is bright green. The silver-gray seed heads persist right through the winter months. Allow it to ramble through a medium-sized shrub or grow it as a specimen plant supported by a single pole or tripod. Pruning is not essential. If necessary, hard-prune in early spring but the flowering will be delayed.
Flowering season: late spring to mid-autumn.
Height: 5 ft (1.5 m).
Zones: 4–9.

Other Species

Clematis tangutica 'Golden Tiara'
1996

Raised and named by Kuif of Uithoorn, Holland and introduced to the British Isles by Pennells Nurseries of Lincoln. The bright yellow flowers with dark purple stamens are borne in great profusion. The plant has attractive seed heads.
Flowering season: midsummer to early autumn.
Height: 5¾–10 ft (1.8– 3 m).
Zones: 4–9.

Clematis rehderiana
1898

A native of western China, collected by Père George Aubert, who introduced it to France in 1898. It was apparently brought to the British Isles (Kew) by Ernest Wilson in 1904. Known as the Nodding Virgin's Bower, this very vigorous woody and deciduous species deserves a place in gardens with space. The stems are angular and downy with rather coarse leaves. Clusters of four-tepalled, bell-shaped, soft, pale primrose-yellow flowers with a gentle primrose scent are produced from the leaf axils in abundance. This is an ideal plant to grow in a large, sunny walled garden of herbs and other fragrant plants. It is best pruned hard each year, although it may be left unpruned if space is not a major criterion.
Flowering season: late summer to mid-autumn.
Height: to 25 ft (7.5 m).
Zones: 6–9.

Clematis rehderiana. Given a sunny spot the clusters of primrose-yellow fragrant flowers distinguish this much loved species.

Clematis potanini var. fargesii

This native of southwestern China is a choice plant, strictly for spacious gardens. It is admirably suited for growing through a strong conifer or any other large evergreen tree or shrub. Small creamy white flowers, about 1½ in. (4 cm) across, are borne singly or in clusters. Welcome small silky seed heads intermingle with the flowers. Pruning is optional. The plant may be simply tidied up or pruned very hard in late winter or early spring.
Flowering season: midsummer to mid-autmn.
Height: over 20 ft (6 m).
Zones: 3–9.

Clematis flammula
1590

Aptly called the Fragrant Virgin's Bower, this species can be variable. It is a Mediterranean plant and prefers well-drained, humus-rich soils. Let it ramble over shrubs, climb up into trees or cover an arbor, flower profusely— there are thousands of blooms on a mature plant—and fill the air with hawthorn-vanilla scent. The four-tepalled flowers are tiny, about 1 in. (2.5 cm) across. Trusses of white, foamy blooms from mid-summer to mid-autumn are a spectacular sight. The plant resents cold and wet summers. However, space permitting, it is a splendid plant and the garden in autumn is much the poorer without its beauty and fragrance. Refrain from overwatering this clematis because it can withstand a certain amount of drought. Pruning is optional. It may be pruned lightly or cut back hard.
Flowering season: late summer to mid-autumn.
Height: 14¾ ft (4.5 m).
Zones: 6–9.

Herbaceous Clematis

Species and Hybrids

Gardeners often associate clematis with climbing or crawling habits and seldom realize there are a number of herbaceous species and hybrids. Some are truly herbaceous, dying back every winter and coming into growth the following spring from rootstocks, while others carry sub-shrubby top growth that breaks into bud along the stems. Herbaceous clematis make very useful plants in perennial borders and, in fact, the famous *Clematis texensis* from North America is herbaceous in its growing habit. Tall, short, or compact, almost all are easy-to-grow and delightful flowering plants with only some requiring a little bit of cosseting. Plant the short and compact varieties among other perennials for companionship and support or assist the stems of the taller ones by growing the plants through or near small or medium-sized shrubs or on suitable supports and tying the stems in.

The cultural requirements of herbaceous clematis are very similar to those of the climbing kinds and most other plants in the garden. Treat them just as you would other perennials in the garden borders and adopt a common-sense approach to cultivating them. Cut back the old flowered stems or the previous year's growths to ground level during late winter or early spring. Mulch and nourish the plants after pruning to encourage emergence of fresh new shoots. Over a period of time they will make large clumps. Plants can be propagated from basal cuttings in spring, by simple division, or by layering. Seed-propagated plants tend to be variable. There is fun and challenge in that too. Who knows, the gardener may be fortunate and grow a seedling or two boasting a special characteristic!

Clematis x aromatica
1855

Possibly introduced to the gardening public by Lemoine of France and probably in existence even before that, this is a semi-herbaceous perennial with somewhat downy, much-branched stems. The dark violet or bluish violet small flowers, 1¼–1½ in. (3–4 cm) in diameter are produced on long stalks and are four-tepalled. The tepals are long and pointed with recurved tips. The central tuft of stamens is whitish cream. The flowers do not freely emit a strong scent as the name would suggest, but on a warm sunny day their vanilla-hawthorn scent may be evident. Plant on a sunny border. Propagate by softwood cuttings, taken during early and mid-summer, or divide established large clumps.
Flowering season: mid-summer to early autumn.
Height: 5 ft (1.5 m).
Zones: 4–9.

Clematis x aromatica is a delightful clematis suitable for a herbaceous or mixed border. Its uncomplicated small pretty flowers are carried on long stalks.

Clematis heracleifolia
1837

This semi-herbaceous species, all the way from China, is variable. It is a strong, stout-stemmed plant with large and coarse leaves producing hyacinth-like narrow tubular purplish blue flowers. The tepals recurve at the tips. The basal stems of this plant are woody and do not die back completely. A large clump-forming clematis.

Flowering season: late summer to early autumn.
Height: 2–3 ft (60–90 cm).
Zones: 5–9.

Clematis heracleifolia var. davidiana
1863

Named in honor of Père David, who discovered it in China, this plant is sweetly scented with indigo-blue hyacinth-like flowers with spreading tepals. It does not form woody basal shoots and is, therefore, more herbaceous in its growing habit. Autumnal sere leaves are fragrant.

Flowering season: mid-summer to early autumn.
Height: 3 ft (90 cm).
Zones: 3–9.

Above:
Clematis integrifolia is a worthwhile herbaceous plant.

Below:
***Clematis heracleifolia* var. *davidiana*.**

Clematis integrifolia
1573

A central European plant introduced into England; this species is an erect herbaceous perennial. The leaves, which have a smooth surface and are slightly hairy underneath, have no stalks. Each stem carries a dark violet or blue pendulous flower made up of four thick tepals which recurve toward the margins. The central tuft of stamens is creamy white and densely packed.

Flowering season: early summer to early autumn.
Height: 2–3 ft (60–90 cm).
Zones: 3–9.

The following named cultivars of *C. integrifolia* are invaluable perennials. They all flower between early summer and early autumn, vary in height between 2–3 ft (60–90 cm), and carry attractive seed heads.

C. i. 'Alba' has white flowers; *C. i.* 'Olgae' has sweetly scented light blue flowers with long and recurved tepals; *C. i.* 'Pastel Pink' has loosely arranged bell-like light pink fragrant flowers; *C. i.* 'Rosea' has sugar-pink and fragrant flowers with twisted tepals crimped along the edges.

Clematis 'Durandii'
1874

Raised in France by Durand Frères. Despite being described as a climber, it makes sense to grow it as a semi-herbaceous perennial. The plant throws up numerous shoots annually from ground level, which grow into tall stems with a clumsy growing habit. The leaves, which resemble those of one of its parents, *C. integrifolia*, the other being *C.* 'Jackmanii,' have no adaptations to wrap around a support. The handsome, well-held, glossy textured flowers are intense indigo blue in color with four, five, or six longitudinally ribbed and irregularly waved tepals with pointed tips. The

dense prominent central tuft of stamens is creamy white. Ideally, it should be grown through a shrub to complement its habit, or be allowed to scramble through other low-growing perennials in a border. Prune back hard each year to ground level. Prone to mildew.

Flowering season: early summer to mid-autumn.
Height: min. 5¾ ft (1.8 m).
Zones: 5–9.

Clematis x jouiniana 'Praecox'

Although this strong-growing hybrid may not be as vigorous as the *montanas*, in common with them it needs space to grow. It is more a sub-shrub and so it forms a woody base. Cut hard back to the woody base instead of ground level. The plant takes a couple of seasons to establish a healthy and strong root system but once established the panicles of flowers are borne in great profusion. The flowers are off-white with an impressive hint of mauvish blue;

Clematis 'Durandii' is one of the best and most popular clematis. The well-shaped deep blue perfect flowers with tight central bundle of white filaments and cream anthers are delightful.

the tepals, reflexed at their tips, number four to six and are long-lasting. On a warm sunny day they are faintly fragrant. A suitable ground cover plant.

Flowering season: early summer to mid-autumn.
Height/spread: 10 ft (3 m).
Zones: 3–9.

Clematis recta var. recta
1597

This plant, indigenous to northern Asia, central and southern Europe, is a variable species, particularly with regard to height, leaf form, and flowering habit. However, be it compact and short or somewhat untidy and tall, it deserves a place in the perennial border, either in the middle or at the back as appropriate. The early stems, deceptively erect, will soon demand a support. Strong pea sticks and hazel stakes are useful supports; alternatively, create a tripod with bamboo canes. The leaves with 5–7 leaflets are deep blue-green. Many terminal clusters of small, starry, four-tepalled and sweetly scented white flowers are borne in great profusion in mid-summer followed by an abundance of decorative seed heads in late summer. Prune the stems hard down to 6 in. (15 cm) in late autumn, although in severely cold regions, pruning can be delayed until the new growth emerges from

below the soil level in spring. The plant will form a large clump with age and can be divided. It is easily propagated from seed. *C. recta* var. *purpurea* is a purple-leafed form of the species. The young growth is deep purple, maturing to green as the plant gets older. This form is much coveted by flower arrangers just for its foliage.
Flowering season: early to mid-summer.
Height: 3–6½ ft (1–2 m).
Zones: 3–9.

Above: The stems of *Clematis recta* var. *recta* are by no means erect and need support. Terminal clusters of starry, sweetly-scented flowers are borne in great profusion.

Left: *Clematis* x *jouiniana* 'Praecox' is a sub-shrub demanding ample space to show off its panicles of off-white, faintly fragrant flowers with an impressive hint of mauvish blue.

Other Recommended Herbaceous Clematis

Clematis 'Eriostemon'
has purple-blue, semi-nodding flowers.
Height: 6½ ft (2 m).

Clematis 'Petit Faucon'
has deep blue, nodding flowers.
Height: 3 ft (1 m).

Clematis 'Aljonushka'
has rich mauve-pink, semi-nodding to nodding, flowers.
Height: 3–5 ft (1–1.5 m).

Clematis heracleifolia 'Cote d'Azur' has pale blue tubular flowers.
Height: 2½ ft (75 cm).

Helpful Hint
Where the plants are tall, it is necessary to give them suitable supports and tie in the stems regularly from the beginning of the growing season.

Connoisseur Collection

As you become more confident and knowledgeable about clematis, you may feel inclined to turn your attention to some of the more unusual, exotic, and neglected species and hybrids. Not all of these are easy to grow, and you may have to seek them out or grow them from seed or cuttings. Taking on the challenge of cultivating and caring for them can be exciting and very rewarding. I have given below the salient features of my personal selection, which I hope you will find useful. Dates of introduction are given where known.

Clematis addisonii

This native of eastern North America (Virginia, North Carolina) grows along wooded river banks. It is a variable low-growing perennial with young blue-green erect branches that become prostrate as they mature. The leaves are sea-green and the pendulous, pitcher-shaped flowers about 1¼ in. (3 cm) across, are borne on long stalks. The four thick and fleshy tepals, recurved at the tips, are rosy purple with creamy inside. The plant is best grown in a warm sunny border. It resents waterlogged sites and too much moisture.
Flowering season: early to mid-summer.
Pruning group: 3.
Height: 2–3 ft (0.6–1 m).
Zones: 7–9.

Clematis alpina ssp. sibirica 'White Moth' is not a very strong growing plant, but it is later flowering than other *alpinas*. The plump buds may not open fully to expose the elegant white tepals.

Clematis aethusifolia
Circa 1860

Slender, ribbed stems characterize this scandent climber from North China. The bright green leaves are very finely cut, giving a lace effect. Small pendulous, bell-shaped flowers, about ¾ in. (2 cm) across, are borne in threes and fives from the top part of the current year's growth on erect stalks. The four narrow tepals with pointed recurved tips are prominently ribbed and pale primrose-yellow to cream-white. Seedheads are fluffy with white-plumose seedtails. This clematis is best grown over a medium-sized open shrub or in a large container. It requires good drainage.
Flowering season: mid-summer to early autumn.
Pruning group: 3.
Height: 6½ ft (2 m).
Zones: 5–9.

Clematis afoliata
Rush-stemmed Clematis 1871

This semi-scandent, almost leafless, shrub from New Zealand has wire-like, slender, smooth, dark green stems and many side branches with branchlets. Over a period of time it will grow into a large interwoven mass of stems. Minute triangular leaflets may be present in the leaves of young plants. The flowers, 1 in. (2.5 cm) across, are borne singly or in groups of two to six. The four to six open or spreading tepals are pale yellow with a greenish shading and silky on the outside. Flower stalks are slim and pubescent. Seed heads are composed of reddish brown achenes with almost silky seed tails. This is a half-hardy species, requiring a warm sheltered wall or cool greenhouse.
Flowering season: mid to late spring.
Pruning group: 1.
Height: 6½–10 ft (2–3 m).
Zones: 8–9.

Clematis alpina var. sibirica (syn. C. sibirica)

In its natural habitat in northern Norway and Finland to East Siberia, the Central Ural Mountains and Manchuria, this smooth-stemmed plant grows between granite rocks and debris. The leaves are pale green and coarse with margins notched like a saw but with irregular teeth. Juvenile leaves are almost yellow-green. The solitary, pendulous, bell-like flowers, about 2 in. (5 cm) long, are not very open. They have four bright white tepals, much longer than broad, shaped like a lance-head and tapering to points with slightly concave sides. The staminodes (sterile stamens), are white, spatula-shaped, and downy. There are many seed heads. The achenes boast silky seed tails. This clematis is best grown through medium-sized shrubs or tumbling over low walls.

Flowering season: mid to late spring.
Pruning group: 1 (Not very vigorous, prune only when necessary).
Height: 5–6½ ft (1.5–2 m).
Zones: 3–9.

Clematis addisonii. The sea-green leaves and the small pendent flowers composed of thick, fleshy rosy-purple tepals are in a class of their own.

Clematis cirrhosa 'Jingle Bells' 1995

This evergreen seedling of *C. cirrhosa* 'Freckles' was raised by the nursery grower Robin Savill. The leaves are somewhat larger than those of the species *cirrhosa*, and the flowers are much more noticeable than in the species. Cream colored buds open to small pure white bell-shaped flowers. A well-drained soil and sunny south-facing aspect are needed for the plant to flower well.

Flowering season: late autumn to early winter.
Pruning group: 1.
Height: 20 ft (6 m).
Zones: 7–9.

Clematis coactilis

The whole of this low-growing herbaceous plant from North America is covered in soft white down, just like the very young leaves of Lamb's Ears (*Stachys lanata*). The young shoots are handsome and silky in appearance. The leaves are simple, sessile, and light green. Small, nodding, pitcher-shaped flowers, borne singly at stem tips and leaf axils, are held on erect long stalks. The four creamy white tepals have recurved, slightly pinkish, tips. The plant is hardy and suitable for a rockery. It needs good drainage and gritty soil.

Flowering season: late spring to early summer.
Pruning group: 3.
Height: 1–1½ ft (30–45m).
Zones: 5–9.

Clematis columbiana var. columbiana

Often confused with *C. occidentalis* and also referred to as *C. pseudoalpina* because of its similarities to the European *C. alpina*, *C. columbiana* is a species occurring from western Montana to northern Arizona and New Mexico, Utah and Colorado. It is a semi-woody deciduous scrambler with slender branchlets. The leaves are twice ternate, that is, the three primary divisions are again divided into three parts and therefore composed of nine leaflets, toothed, lobed, or further dissected, giving a fern-like appearance. Flowers are solitary and nodding and borne on the previous year's wood. The four tepals are translucent blue, wider at the base, and tapering to pointed tips. The plant is listed in the RHS *Plant Finder*, along with *C. occidentalis*. Be sure to get the correct plant: the difference between the two species lies in the leaves. *C. occidentalis* has ternate leaves, that is, leaves divided into three parts, rather than twice ternate leaves. Container cultivation is recommended for this rare plant.

Flowering season: mid to late spring.
Pruning group: 1.
Height: 2–3 ft (60–90 cm).
Zones: 3–9.

Clematis crispa
Blue Jasmine, Marsh Clematis, or Curly Clematis
1726

This slender, not very vigorous, deciduous climber with a herbaceous habit is from the southeastern United States, where it grows in swamps and similar habitats. Its fine dainty leaves are divided into five to seven small, smooth, ovate leaflets, which are usually simple and entire with three apparent veins from the base. The small flowers, ¾–1 ½ in. (2–4 cm) long, are solitary, pendulous, and bell-shaped and held on long stalks measuring 3 in. (7.5 cm). The four blue or blue-purple tepals are jointed at the base but spreading and at times twisted at the tips and recurving right back to touch the outside, with margins crisped or undulate above the middle. Seed heads and flowers appear together. This clematis is readily propagated from seed and merits a place in the garden. It is suitable for growing over a small to medium shrub. Flowers are not produced

in abundance. It is generally hardy but protection for the root crown during winter is recommended.
Flowering season: early summer to early autumn.
Pruning group: 3.
Height: 6½–8 ft (2–2.5 m).
Zones 6–9.

Clematis 'Edward Prichard'
1950

This herbaceous variety with slender arching stems was raised by Russell Pritchard in Australia, from a cross between *C. recta* x *C. heracleifolia*

Clematis crispa. **Not very vigorous, herbaceous in habit, the divided leaves, solitary bell-shaped flowers with slightly spreading and recurved tepals held on long stalks make this species a very special plant.**

'Davidiana.' The leaves are divided into five leaflets, irregularly lobed and coarsely serrated. The fragrant, cross-shaped flowers, 1½ in. (4 cm) across, are white, shading to mauve-pink, and deepening toward the tips. They have creamy white stamens. The plant is best grown in full sun over a low-growing dark conifer or cotoneaster. It is ideal for tumbling over a low

retaining wall. Everett Leeds, a former Chairman of the British Clematis Society, informed the author that the flowers do not produce viable seed.
Flowering season: mid to late summer.
Pruning group: 3 (can be tidied up in autumn if necessary).
Height: 3 ft (1 m).
Zones: 5–9.

Clematis finetiana

A semi-evergreen species from central and west China. It is not a vigorous climber but requires a warm, sunny, and sheltered site to climb well and flower. The leaves, composed of three leaflets (trifoliate), are thin, leathery, smooth, and bright green with three distinct veins. The flowers are carried on main inflorescence stalks in clusters of three, or at times seven, borne in the axils. They are star-like when fully open, about 1½ in. (4 cm) across, with four white, smooth, spreading tepals, shaped like lanceheads and pointed at the tips. This fine plant is moderately hardy in mild and sheltered maritime gardens and makes a good conservatory plant in colder regions.
Flowering season: late spring to early summer.
Pruning group: 1.
Height: 10–13 ft (3–4 m).
Zones: 8–9.

Clematis florida

This very rare plant, originally found in its native habitat in China by Augustine Henry, is either lost in the wild or at least has not been seen recently, according to Raymond Evison. The author has seen two plants in flower, one in Ruth Gooch's Thorncroft Clematis Nursery, Norwich and the other in the Oxford garden of Mike Brown, Chairman of the British Clematis Society. Both are sports from *C. florida* 'Sieboldii' reverting to *C. florida* and are container-grown under glass. It is a deciduous climber and has tough and wiry stems. The leaves are divided into three leaflets, tapering at both ends, much longer than broad, and wider below the middle part. Flowers, produced in abundance from the axils, are solitary, flat, and about 3–4 in. (7.5–10 cm) wide. Flower stalks have a pair of heart-shaped leaf-like structures (bracts) without stalks about half way down. There are usually six, sometimes four, rounded white tepals, tapering to points with slightly concave sides and overlapping. They may have a tinted green bar on the underside. The stamens are very striking and spreading. White filaments carry deep violet-black anthers. The seed heads are composed of achenes with silky plume-like seed tails.
Flowering season: late spring to late summer.
Pruning group: 3.
Height: 5¾–8 ft (1.8–2.5 m).
Zones: 6–9.

Clematis florida 'Plena': the many sumptuously double flowers may be heavy for the slender stems but with a distinctly green hue they are quite spectacular. Merits a place in the specialist's collection.

Clematis florida 'Plena'
1835

This spectacular deciduous climber is from Japan. It is a weak-growing plant with slender stems. The rosette-like, sumptuous double flowers, nearly 4 in. (10 cm) across, are sterile. Six overlapping outer protective tepals unfold first to reveal the tightly packed central dome of staminodes, which are the layers of numerous petal-like structures giving the flower the full double form. The outer tepals gradually wither away, leaving the rest of the layers of tepals to open gradually over a long period of time. The greenish white tepals are wide at the base, but narrow toward pointed tips. The thin stems should be fully supported to carry the rather heavy double flowers. 'Plena' is best grown in a container under glass. It makes a splendid patio plant in sheltered gardens. The flowers look good in flower arrangements.
Flowering season: early summer to early or mid-autumn.
Pruning group: 2.
Height: 5¾–8 ft (1.8–2.5 m).
Zones: 7–9.

Clematis florida 'Sieboldii'
(formerly *C. florida* 'Bicolor' and *C. florida* 'Sieboldiana')
1835

Introduced from Japan by Philipp F. von Siebold, this is a much admired climber, similar in its growth habit to *C. florida* and *C. florida* 'Plena.' It has a long flowering period. The sterile flowers are composed of six off-white outer overlapping and gently recurved tepals with pointed tips. A central prominent mass of purple petal-like stamens brings character and drama to the flower. The stems of the plant carry these central domes of flowers for a few days after the outer tepals have fallen away. Occasionally the flowers have a tendency to revert fully or partially to those of *C. florida* 'Plena.' 'Sieboldii' is best grown as a container plant in a conservatory or glasshouse. The flowers look exceptionally good when the plant is trained through the foliage and flowers of *Indigofera heterantha*, or a similar small to medium-sized shrub planted against a warm wall in sheltered gardens in mild areas.
Flowering season: late spring to early or mid-autumn in a conservatory or greenhouse; early summer to mid-autumn in the open garden.
Pruning group: 2 or 3.
Height: 5¾–10 ft (1.8–3 m).
Zones: 7–9.

Clematis forsteri

An evergreen species from New Zealand with male and female flowers on separate plants (dioecious). A plant with male flowers is recommended. It is quite a good climber and requires a warm, sunny, and sheltered site. The bright green, smooth, leathery leaves are composed of three leaflets with toothed margins. Lemon-scented, partially nodding flowers, 1½ in. (4 cm) across, are borne in clusters and in great profusion, almost smothering the leaves. The four (to six) creamy greenish yellow tepals are smooth and silky, open and almost spreading. This is a moderately hardy plant in mild localities and will come through the winter if given a warm, sunny, and sheltered wall. It makes an excellent cool greenhouse or conservatory plant.
Flowering season: mid to late spring.
Pruning group: 1 (may be tidied, if necessary, immediately after flowering).
Height: 6½–10 ft (2–3 m).
Zones: 8–9.

Clematis fusca var. *fusca*
1860

The distribution of this wild species is from Siberia to Japan. It is a herbaceous or semi-woody climber. The leaves are composed of five to seven oval leaflets, wider toward the stalk, some broadly lobed. Urn-shaped, pendulous flowers, ¾–1¼ in. (2–3 cm) long, are borne singly on thick stalks from the axils. The four thick, dark purple tepals, recurved at the tips, are covered with thick, woolly dark brown hairs, giving an overall color of matt dark brown. They are cream-colored on the inside. The rather unusual flowers arouse the curiosity of gardeners and non-gardeners alike and the plant is well worth a place in the garden. Children find the flowers fascinating. Because of its very dark brown color, take care to site this plant against a light background and if growing over a small to medium-sized shrub, opt for a silver-grey or even gold-leaved plant. Alternatively, it may be grown as a container plant against a white wall of the house. There are some clones, which grow only to 3–5 ft (1–1.5 m). The large seed heads are notable. Propagation from seed is easy.
Flowering season: early to late summer.
Pruning group: 3.
Height: 6½–10 ft (2–3 m).
Zones: 5–9.

The novel shaped cluster of flowers of *Clematis fusca* var. *violacea* is a curiosity in the clematis garden. It also has very attractive seed heads.

Clematis fusca var. *violacea*

This variant of the species from Korea and China is similar in many respects. The slightly larger flowers, 1½–2 in. (4–5 cm) across, are borne in clusters of three; without the dense coating of hairs they are more purply bronze in color. The four tepals, recurved at the tips, are purplish blue inside. Large seed heads turn orange with age.
Flowering season: early to late summer.
Pruning group: 3.
Height: 6½–10 ft (2–3 m).
Zones: 5–9.

Clematis heracleifolia var. *davidiana* 'Wyevale'
Circa 1955

Wyevale Nurseries in England raised this very fragrant form of the species *C. heracleifolia*. It is a woody herbaceous non-climbing sub-shrub, which forms a thick clump and sometimes self-layers. The leaves are divided into three parts and are coarsely veined. Hyacinth-like, deep mid-blue flowers, about 1¼ in. (3 cm) across, are produced from the leaf axils on the top half of each stem. This is an excellent mixed-border plant.
Flowering season: late summer to early autumn.
Pruning group: 3.
Height: 3–4 ft (90 cm–1.2m).
Zones: 5–9.

Clematis hirsutissima var. scottii (syn. *C. douglasii* var. 'Scottii')
Circa 1880

A species found growing in the Bad Lands and Black Hills of South Dakota, and in the central and southern Rocky Mountain region of North America and Canada.

It is herbaceous in habit. Young shoots covered in down turn smooth with age. The grayish green leaves are composed of leaflets, which are narrow and much longer than broad, and wider below the middle. The underside is covered in hairs. The flowers are about 1½ in. (4 cm) long and 1¼ in. (3cm) wide; they are pitcher-shaped (urceolate), pendulous, and produced at the top of each shoot. Flower stalks are long. A mature plant displaying its many flowers is a glorious sight. The four thick, downy, pale blue-lavender tepals have a pinkish tinge and are prominently recurved at the tips. The plant is best grown in a sunny border or rock garden; good drainage is essential. It can be grown in a container in good gritty compost. Refrain from over-nourishing if you want it to flower well. Protect the rootcrown during winter. The plant takes a long time to establish, grow, and flower. Seed will germinate successfully but may take three to five years to grow and establish as flowering plants. Patience is vital.

Flowering season: late spring to early summer.
Pruning group: 3 but, being herbaceous, throws up shoots from the soil.
Height: 1½–2 ft (45–60cm)
Zones: 6–9.

Clematis forsteri is not a plant for very cold frosty gardens. Delightful evergreen plant for a sunny wall.

Clematis napaulensis
1912

Native to North India and southwestern China, this clematis is quite a vigorous climber. Leaves, green in winter, are shed in summer during dormancy, and followed by new bright green leaves in or around mid-autumn. Pendulous, somewhat narrow, bell-shaped flowers appear in groups from the leaf axils. The four very pale yellow tepals are recurved at the tips. The stamens, protruding beyond the tepals, are very prominent, rich purple, and contrast elegantly with the creamy white styles and stigmas. The plant is hardy only in mild areas and even then must be given a sheltered, warm, south-facing aspect. Otherwise, it makes an excellent cool conservatory or greenhouse plant. Keep the plant moist but refrain from watering it excessively during summer.

Flowering season: early to late winter.
Pruning group: 1.
Height: 14¾–20 ft (4–6 m).
Zones: 8–9.

Clematis paniculata

Native of New Zealand, this species is variable. Male and female flowers are carried on separate plants (dioecious). Invest in a male plant—the flowers are much larger than those of female forms and boast central bosses of salmon-pink anthers. In its native habitat, this species grows up and over trees, displaying its clusters of gleaming white flowers during early spring. It is an evergreen climber. The glossy, thick, and leathery leaves are typically composed of three leaflets that often have one or two pairs of notches near the tips. The leaf margins are wavy. Gently nodding, flat flowers, 2–3 in. (5–7.5 cm) across, are composed of six to eight gleaming white tepals. They are borne in leaf axils in great profusion, almost hiding the foliage.

The plant is hardy only in mild areas and, even then, best given a sunny south-facing sheltered wall. Be sure greedy snails do not devour the young new shoots and flower buds. It makes a fine conservatory or cool greenhouse plant.

Flowering season: mid-spring to early summer.
Pruning group: 1.
Height: 10–12 ft (3–3.6m).
Zones: 7–9.

Clematis phlebantha
1952

In the wild, this Himalayan species, first discovered in western Nepal, grows in low-rainfall areas on dry, sun-baked cliffs and exposed rocky hillsides between 8,200 and 12,100 ft (2,500–3,700 m). It is a sprawling, shrubby plant with excellent neat silvery leaves that are dissected and potentilla-like and densely covered in short fine hairs. The white, flat and open flowers, borne singly in axils, are set off most effectively against the leaves. The tepals, usually six, are delicately veined (the plant takes its name from the Greek word, *phlebos*, meaning "vein"), pointed and somewhat spreading. According to Tony Schilling, best known for his plant introductions from the Himalayas, propagation is relatively easy under mist from cuttings taken in late summer. The plant is not very hardy and is best grown as a conservatory or cool greenhouse plant.

Flowering season: early to late summer.
Pruning Group: 2.
Height: 3–5 ft (1–1.5 m).
Zones: 8–9.

Clematis texensis
1868

The only true red species is found growing along streams and in woods, on the Edwards Plateau of Texas and extending into northeastern Texas. Formerly known as *Clematis coccinea*, it is thought to have been introduced to Europe in 1868. The German botanist Max Leichtlin introduced the species to England in 1880. It is a herbaceous perennial, with slender, ribbed, smooth, sea-green stems. The slender leaf axils are abruptly bent and terminated by a tendril-like structure. Leaves are made up of four to five pairs of leaflets with rounded to heart-shaped bases, short sharp points, and a fine network of veins. Scarlet-red, pitcher-shaped flowers, ¾–1¼ in. (2–3 cm) long and partially nodding, are carried on stalks which are ribbed and colored red. The four thick tepals are roughly oval in outline, wider toward the stalk, and narrowing toward the recurved tips. The margins are scarcely expanded, white, and densely covered in short fine hairs, giving a cottony matted finish. The seed heads are large, the achene bodies are disc-shaped, symmetrical, prominently rimmed, and the seed tails are feathery and yellowish brown. This is a much sought after species, but not easy to cultivate; it is difficult to propagate from cuttings. Most plants are grown from seed, layers, or by division. It is prone to mildew, a trait often seen in many of its hybrids, perhaps with the exception of *C. texensis* 'Princess Diana.' It is best grown as a container plant but may be grown in the open garden through a small to medium-sized silver or gray-leaved shrub.

Flowering season: early summer to early or mid-autumn.
Pruning group: 3.
Height: 5–6½ ft (1.5–2 m).
Zones: 4–9.

Opposite: *Clematis texensis* **is a much sought-after species. Although not all that easy to cultivate, the exquisite scarlet red, pitcher shaped flowers are unique.**

Below: *Clematis viorna* **has violet to reddish purple nodding flowers which are borne on stiff stalks. Spider-like seed heads are large in spite of the small flowers.**

Clematis viorna
Leather Flower or Vase Vine
1753

This herbaceous climbing plant is found growing on wooded riverbanks and in similar habitats, in the Piedmont and mountain regions from southern Pennsylvania to northern Mississippi, and from Ohio west to southern Missouri.

The stems are slender, angular, and hairy below the nodes. Leaves consist of five to seven roughly oval, deep green leaflets, the terminal pair of which are usually minute. Leaves end in a slender tendril-like structure. The violet to reddish purple flowers, carried on stiff stalks, are nodding, more or less oval in shape, urn-like, and ¾–1 in. (2–2.5 cm) long. The four thick tepals with smooth woolly recurved tips, equal or slightly exceed the length of the stamens. The margins are creamy white and not expanded. Seed heads are spider-like, large, and composed of achenes with conspicuously rimmed bodies and light yellow-brownish feathery seed tails that are spreading or loosely coiled. A dainty clematis to grow over a prostrate or low-growing conifer or medium-sized shrub of contrasting color. It may also be grown over a low stone wall or in a container. It grows readily from seed.

Flowering season: early to mid-summer.
Pruning group: 3.
Height: 6½–8 ft (2–2.5 m).
Zones: 4–9.

Exhibiting and Choosing Clematis

Bibliography, Glossary and Index

Exhibiting Clematis

Most clematis are climbers and are not ideally suited for exhibiting unless, of course, they are young container-grown plants. However, there are a number of slow-growing compact plants, including the New Zealand species and hybrids, which can be trained and exhibited at shows. The Alpine Society shows invariably feature some well-grown clematis, for example, *Clematis marmoraria*, *C.* x *cartmanii* 'Joe', *C.* 'Moonman', *C.* 'majojo', *C.* 'Lunar Lass'. If you have never exhibited a clematis, visit some major shows to get some ideas on how to grow and present your plants.

Before you decide to grow a plant for exhibition, it is important to obtain a show schedule well in advance, even one from the previous year will do. There are rules and regulations governing the pot size and other requirements. There will be very little point in growing a beautiful clematis in a very large pot if the class in which you wish to exhibit clearly states that the maximum container size is 6 in. (15 cm).

Plan well ahead of time. If you are starting from seed, cuttings, or "liners," the plants will need time to grow—at least two or three seasons. Choose the clematis you wish to exhibit carefully, particularly with regard to its flowering time. Timing is absolutely critical because you need the display of flowers exactly on the day of the

Clematis 'Warsaw Nike' (syn. *C.* 'Warszawska Nike') is a good Polish cultivar raised by Brother Stefan Franczak. It creates drama in the garden with rich velvety red-purple flowers with contrasting pale yellow anthers.

show itself. Only by trial and error will you know the actual time of flowering. This will also depend on the conditions under which your plants are growing. If the weather is unusually cold for the time of the year when your plant should be in flower, a little bit of heat in a greenhouse or conservatory may help to bring forward the flowering time. If the weather is unseasonably warm, then you must try and delay the buds rushing into flowers: bringing the plant into a well-lit cold room could do the trick. The important tip is, do not feed your clematis once the buds are plump.

It will also be helpful to know what criteria the judges use in awarding points for an exhibit. There are different rules for different societies, and they may vary from country to country. The overall appearance of the plant and the cleanliness of the container are paramount. Take some time to remove withered, brown, or dead leaves from the plant. If a cane supports it, ensure that the plant is bushy and that the foliage and flowers hide as much of the support as is possible. If the plant is compact and low-growing, top-dressing the surface of the compost with attractive horticultural grit will enhance the appearance of the exhibit. The plant must carry the correct botanical name written legibly on a label.

I am full of admiration for the dedicated gardeners who spend a considerable amount of time growing their plants to absolute perfection year after year for exhibiting at shows. They also seem to cope well with the vagaries of weather, particularly during spring.

For information on planting, growing, pinching out the tips of the growing shoots to make the plants bushy, and pruning, read the chapter on Cultivating Clematis (page 20).

Choosing Clematis

The following lists of species and hybrids are by no means definitve and are intended to assist you in choosing your clematis by color and for different places and uses in the garden. Among some of the large-flowered hybrids the differences between one named variety and another may be negligble or insignificant. Therefore, the very best tried and tested varieties are included in the list. With regard to suitable locations for clematis, some north-facing aspects and windy sites are more hospitable than others.

Best Clematis by Color

Pink
'Asao'
'Charissima'
'Comtesse de Bouchaud'
'Dr. Ruppel'
'Dorothy Walton'
'Hagley Hybrid'
'John Warren'
'Madame Baron Veillard'
'Margaret Hunt'
'Pink Fantasy'

Red
'Allanah'
'Barbara Dibley'
'Cardinal Wysznski'
'Crimson King'
'Ernest Markham'
'Jackmanii Rubra'
'Madame Edouard André'
'Niobe'
'Rouge Cardinal'
'Ville de Lyon'

White/cream
'Edith'
'Gillian Blades'
'Guernsey Cream'
'Henryi'
'Huldine'
'John Huxtable'
'Marie Boisselot'
'Miss Bateman'
'Snow Queen'
'Wada's Primrose'

Early Blue-purple
'Fujimusume'
'H. F. Young'
'Lady Northcliffe'
'Lasurstern'
'Lord Nevill'
'Mrs. Cholmondeley'
'Richard Pennell'
'The President'
'W. E. Gladstone'
'William Kennett'

Late blue-purple
'Ascotiensis'
'Gipsy Queen'
'Jackmanii Superba'
'Jackmanii'
'Lady Betty Balfour'
'Madame Grangé'
'Perle d'Azur'
'Prince Charles'
'Star of India'
'Victoria'

Best Striped Clematis

'Barbara Jackman'
'Bee's Jubilee'
'Captaine Thuilleaux'
'Corona'
'Dr. Ruppel'
'Fair Rosamond'
'Mrs. N. Thompson'
'Nellie Moser'
'Sealand Gem'
'Star of India'

Best Double Clematis

'Arctic Queen'
'Daniel Deronda'
'Duchess of Edinburgh'
florida 'Alba Plena'
'Josephine'
'Louise Rowe'
'Multi Blue'
'Patricia Ann Fretwell'
'Proteus'
'Sylvia Denny'
'Veronica's Choice'
'Vyvyan Pennell'

Best Herbaceous and Semi-Herbaceous Clematis

'Aljonushka'
'Durandii'
'Petit Faucon'
x *aromatica*
heracleifolia 'Stans'
heracleifolia var. davidiana 'Wyevale'
integrifolia 'Alba'
integrifolia 'Rosea'

Best Scented Clematis

x *aromatica*
x *triternata* 'Rubromarginata'
flammula
heracleifolia var. davidiana 'Wyevale'
montana 'Elizabeth'
montana var. *wilsonii*
rehderiana

Best Clematis for Different Locations

Exposed north walls, fences, and windy sites

All *alpina, macropetala,* and *tangutica* types.

Sheltered north walls with good light

All *alpina, macropetala, tangutica,* and
'Bee's Jubilee'
'Carnaby'
'Comtesse de Bouchaud'
'Dawn'
'Dr. Ruppel'
'Guernsey Cream'
'Hagley Hybrid'
'Henryi'
'John Warren'
'Nelly Moser'

South or southwest aspect (Evergreens)

armandii 'Apple Blossom'
cirrhosa balearica
cirrhosa 'Freckles'
forsteri
paniculata

South or west aspect (Doubles and semi-doubles)

'Arctic Queen'
'Daniel Deronda'
'Kathleen Dunford'
'Mrs. George Jackman'
'Mrs. James Mason'
'Multi Blue'
'Royalty'
'Vyvyan Pennell' and other double and semi-double varieties.

South or west aspect (Large-flowered hybrids)

Any white, blue, deep blue, purple, or red and the following grow and flower best given a south or west-facing position.
'Ernest Markham'
'Lady Betty Balfour'
'Lord Nevill'
'Mrs. Hope'
'Prins Hendrik'

East-facing aspect

Any species or hybrids excluding those mentioned under south, southwest, or west-facing aspects.

Best clematis for growing in association with small trees and shrubs

'Comtesse de Bouchaud'
'Dorothy Walton'
'Duchess of Sutherland'
'Etoile de Malicorne'
'Gipsy Queen'
'Henryi'
'Huldine'
'Jackmanii Alba'
'Jackmanii Superba'
'Marie Boisselot'
'Miss Bateman'
'Ramona'
x *eriostemon* 'Hendersonii' and small-flowered alpina, macropetala and viticella types.

Best clematis for growing on poles, arches, pergolas in association with other climbing plants and roses

'Arabella'
'Ascotiensis'
'Comtesse de Bouchaud'
'Elsa Spath'
'General Sikorski'
'Mrs. Cholmondeley'
'Perle d'Azur'
'Star of India'
'Victoria'
'Ville de Lyon'
'William Kennett'
viticella 'Betty Corning'
viticella 'Etoile Violette'
viticella 'Polish Spirit'
viticella 'Venosa Violocea'

Best clematis for a conservatory

aethusifolia
florida 'Alba Plena'
florida 'Sieboldii'
forsteri
marmoraria
napaulensis

Best clematis for containers

'Anna Louise'
'Arctic Queen'
'Asao'
'Dawn'
'Fujimusume'
'H. F. Young'
'Marie Boisselot'
'Mrs. P. B. Truax'
'Niobe'
'Pink Fantasy'
'Silver Moon'
'Sunset'
'Vino'
x *aromatica*
alpina 'Pink Flamingo'
macropetala 'Lagoon'

Author's choice for small urban gardens

'Arctic Queen'
'Durandii'
'Fujimusume'
'Hagley Hybrid'
'Miss Bateman'
'Niobe'
'Petit Faucon'
'Pink Fantasy'
'Romantika'
'Sylvia Denny'
'The Vagabond'
x *aromatica*
alpina 'Helsingborg'
alpina var. ochotensis 'Carmen Rose'
heracleifolia 'Stans'
integrifolia 'Alba'
macropetala 'Maidwell Hall'
macropetala 'Markham's Pink'
macropetala 'White Moth'
texensis 'Princess Diana'
viticella 'Betty Corning'
viticella 'Etoile Violette'
viticella 'Madame Julia Correvon'
viticella 'Margo Koster'
viticella 'Pagoda'

And finally the montanas. These are vigorous plants and need lots of growing space. In my opinion the best of the montanas are: 'Broughton Star,' 'Elizabeth,' 'Freda,' and 'Warwickshire Rose.'

Bibliography

BUCHAN, U. *Wall Plants & Climbers: the National Trust Guide*, Pavilion, 1992

BURRAS, J.K., & Griffiths, M. (ed.) *The New RHS Dictionary, Manual of Climbers and Wall Plants.* pp. 54 -71, Macmillan, 1994

ERICKSON, R.O. "Taxonomy of Clematis section *Viorna*." *Annals of the Missouri Botanical Garden*, 30 (1): 1-62, February 1943

EVISON, R.J. *The Gardener's Guide to Growing Clematis*, David & Charles, 1998

FISK, J. *Clematis: the Queen of Climbers*, Cassell, 1994

FRETWELL, B. *Clematis*, Harper Collins, 1989

GOOCH, R. *Clematis: the Complete Guide*, Crowood Press, 1996

HALL, N., NEWDICK., J. & SUTHERLAND, N. *Growing Clematis*, Aura Books, 1994

HOWELLS, J. *The Rose and the Clematis as good companions*, Garden Art Press, 1996

JACKMAN, A.G. "Hybrid Clematis," *JRHS* 24: 315, 1900

JOHNSON, M. *Släktet Klematis (The Genus Clematis)* Magnus Johnson's Plantskola AB, Södertälje, Sweden, 1996

LAMB, J.G.D. *The Propagation of Climbing Clematis*, Plantsman 12(3): 178 -80, 1990

LLOYD, C. *Clematis* (revised edition with T. Bennett), Viking, 1989

MARKHAM, E. *Clematis*, Country Life, 1935

MOORE, T. and JACKMAN, G. *The Clematis as a Garden Flower*, John Murray, 1872

ROBINSON, W. *The Virgin's Bower*, John Murray, 1912

SNOEIJER, W. *Clematis Index*, Boskoop: J. Fopma, 1991

TOOMEY, M.K. (ed). *The Clematis: Journal of the British Clematis Society*, 1995-1998

TOOMEY, M.K. "Notes on *Clematis x aromatica*." *The New Plantsman* 4 (2) 79-82, 1997

WHITEHEAD, S.B. *Garden Clematis*, The Trinity Press, 1959

Useful Addresses

American Clematis Society
P.O. Box 17085, Irvine, California 92623-7085
  http://clematis.org

British Clematis Society (Secretary: Richard Stothard)
  4 Springfield, Lightwater, Surrey GU18 5XP, UK

International Clematis Society
(Registrar: Victoria Matthews)
  7350 SW 173rd Street, Miami, Florida 33157-4835
  http://dspace/dial/pipex.com/town/terrace/pk91

John Maskelyne, BCS Trial Grounds Coordinator,
  5 Brookside, Moulton, Newmarket, Suffolk,
  CB8 8SG, UK

Glossary

Achene
A dry fruit enclosing a single seed. A number of achenes are held together and form a single seed head in clematis.

Anther
The swollen part (head) of a stamen which carries the pollen .

Axil
The angle between a leaf stalk and the stem of a plant. A bud that develops in the leaf axil is called an axillary bud or a side bud.

Bisexual
Having male and female parts in the same flower.

Biternate
Description of a leaf divided into three parts which in turn are again divided into three.

Calyx
The outermost part or whorl of a flower. It is usually green in color. (See sepal.)

Chlorosis
A term applied to leaves when they become pale green in color, or even yellow, due to magnesium deficiency. Iron or manganese deficiency can also cause chlorosis.

Chromosomal number
Chromosomes (hereditary material) consist of DNA and carry the genetic code for a living organism. The number of chromosomes is fixed for each species and is useful for plant or animal identification.

Clone
A genetically uniform collection of plants reproduced by asexual vegetative methods, such as layering and cuttings (as distinct from being propagated from seed), from a single parent.

Compound
A term used to describe a leaf consisting of separate leaflets which are held together by leafstalks.

Corolla
Inner whorl or part of a flower, composed of petals, usually brightly colored. Seldom green.

Cultivar
Word formed from CULTIvated VARiety and applied to a plant (hybrid) deliberately bred or selected and not found growing in the wild. *Clematis florida* 'Sieboldii' is an example. Note the cultivar 'Sieboldii' is set in Roman type within single quotation marks, while the generic and specific names are set in italics.

Dioecious
Male and female flowers on separate plants.

Downy (leaf)
Covered with short stiff hairs.

Filament
A fine stem that carries the anther in a stamen.

Flower stalk
Also known as the pedicel, it is the stem that supports the flower or the flowerhead.

Genus
A unit or category of botanic classification. A group of species of plants which are closely related forms a genus (plural, genera).

Glaucous (leaf)
Green tinged with strong bluish green; covered with a grayish waxy bloom.

Habit
A term used to describe the general appearance of a plant—including its climbing, trailing, or erect growth pattern—and other features so that it can be easily recognized.

Hard prune
To cut back a plant to within a few buds from the base on shoots above the ground, in order to promote vigorous growth.

Herbaceous
In garden terms, used to describe the habit of plants, mostly perennials, which die down at the end of a growing season and return to full growth above the ground level the following spring. In botanical usage, the term also applies to annuals and biennials .

Hybrid
A term given to a plant obtained by crossing two different species. Hybrids seldom breed true and some are even sterile. Synonymous with cultivar.

Hybridization
A method used by plant breeders to produce new hybrids and achieved by controlled cross-pollina-tion, in which pollen from one plant is transferred to another plant with the aid of a brush.

Inflorescence
Arrangement of flowers on a shoot, branch or a stem in a simple grouping or a definite flower-cluster.

Internode
That portion of the stem between two consecutive nodes (leaf joints).

Internodal cuttings
Cuttings taken between the nodes and not trimmed back to a leaf joint (node). A method of vegetative propagation.

Layering
A method of vegetative propagtion, carried out by burying a part of a stem while it is still attached to the parent plant.

Liner
A term used in the nursery trade for a young plant in its first pot and not ready for planting out in the garden.

Node
A point where the leaf is attached to the stem, also known as the leaf joint.

Pedicel
Flower stalk.

Petaloid stamens
Modified stamens with petal-like appearance in color and texture.

Petiole
Slender stalk by which a leaf is attached to the stem; leafstalk

Pubescent
Hairy or downy—often used to describe leaves or buds covered with short, soft hairs.

Sepal
A component of calyx. Usually green and leaf-like. Sometimes sepals become brightly colored like the petals or even replace the petals.

Sere
Dried or withered.

Simple
Description of a leaf not divided into leaflets.

Solitary
A term used to describe flowers when they appear singly, as opposed to in clusters.

Species
Basic unit of biological classification. A group of very closely related plants that can interbreed freely with one another, and breed true, but not usually with members of another species. If they do the resulting hybrids will be infertile.

Stamen
Male reproductive part of a flower, made up of a filament and anther.

Staminode
An infertile stamen (no pollen).

Stigma
Found at the tip of a pistil (female reproductive part). Serves as receptive surface for pollen.

Tepal
When there is no clear differentiation between a sepal (calyx) and a petal (corolla) the term tepal is used as in Clematis, Magnolia, Tulip, Crocus.

Ternate
A term used to describe a leaf with three parts (leaflets).

Variety
A group of plants within a species that occurs natu-rally in the wild; they have Latin names. The culti-vated varieties (cultivars) are given vernacular names.

x
A sign used to signify hybridization.

Index

Clematis plants are indexed under the species or cultivar. Other plants are indexed in full.

Page numbers in italics refer to illustrations, and those followed by g refer to a glossary entry.

Photographic
Acknowledgments

Acknowledgments in Source Order

Jacket picture **Octopus Publishing Group**/Andrew Lawson

Bernard Allen 85
Garden Picture Library/Alan Bedding 29
/Andy Bee 12
/John Glover 31
/Alex Scaresbrook 69.
John Glover 113.
Harpur Garden Library/Marcus Harpur Endpapers.
M. Jerard 62.
Andrew Lawson 45, 59 left, 102, 105 Bottom Left.
Jan Lindmark 63
Octopus Publishing Group Ltd. 101
/Jerry Harpur 43
/Andrew Lawson 1, 14, 15, 38, 39, 41, 59 right, 71, 72-73, 75, 76, 77 Top, 77 Bottom, 78, 78 Bottom Right, 79 Top Right, 79 Bottom Left, 80 right, 80 Top Left, 81, 82, 86 Top Right, 86 Bottom Left, 88, 89, 91 Top Right, 91 Bottom Left, 92 Top Right, Bottom Left, 93 Top, 93 Bottom, 94 Top & Bottom, 95 Bottom, 96, 97, 98 Top Left, 98 Bottom Right, 99 Top Left, 99 Bottom Right, 100 Top Right, 100 Bottom Left, 103 Bottom Right, 104, 105 Top Right, 108, 112, 119
/Sean Myers 2-3, 4-5, 6-7, 8 Top, 8 Center, 8 Bottom, 9, 9 insert bottom left, 10-11, 16, 17, 18 Top, 18 Bottom, 19 Right, 19 Top Left, 19 Center Left, 19 Bottom Left, 20-21, 22 Top, 22 Bottom, 23 left, 23 Top Right, 23 Bottom Right, 24 Top, 24 Center, 24 Bottom, 25 Top, 25 Center, 26 Top, 26 Center, 26 Bottom, 30 left, 30 right, 32, 46-47, 49 Top Left, 49 Top Right, 49 Bottom Left, 49 Bottom Right, 51 Top Left, 51 Top Right, 51 Bottom Left, 51 Bottom Right, 52 left, 52 Right, 53, 54, 56-57, 58 Top, 58 Center, 58 Bottom, 60 Top, 60 Bottom, 61, 64-65, 70, 85 Bottom Left, 87, 95, 103 Top Left, 106-107, 111, 114, 116-117
/Vanessa Luff 35 Top, 35 Center, 35 Bottom, 36.
Photos Horticultural 28, 40, 83/BT 66, 67.
Dr. J. Pringle 109, 115
Harry Smith Collection 90.
M. K. Toomey 44, 110.

Acknowledgments

The author would like to thank Richard Stothard, Everett Leeds, Mike Brown, Dr. Brian Cromie and Jan Lindmark of the British Clematis Society for their assistance during the preparation of this book.

The publishers and the author would like to thank Mike Brown, The Clematis Corner, Shillingford, Oxford-shire and Ruth Gooch, Thorncroft Clematis Nursery, Reymerston, Norwich, Norfolk for their assistance in the photography for this book.